AFTER THE RAIN

AFTER THE RAIN

A Play in Three Acts

by

JOHN BOWEN

FABER AND FABER
24 Russell Square
London

First published in mcmlxvii
by Faber and Faber Limited
24 Russell Square London WC1
Printed in Great Britain by
Latimer Trend & Co Ltd Plymouth

© *1967 by John Bowen*

For
VIVIAN MATALON
and
ALEC McCOWEN

NOTE TO THE READER

Mr. Bowen originally adapted his novel, *After the Rain*, into a play in 1960 at the request of Bryan Bailey, who was then Director of the Belgrade Theatre, Coventry. Two days after receiving the first draft, Mr. Bailey died in a car crash, the project was abandoned, and the play lay about lumpishly, since John Bowen himself was dissatisfied with what he had done. Then, late in 1964, it suddenly came to him that what he had considered an intractable problem of staging was not intractable at all, given one simple premise—which is the premise of the present play. With the knowledge came a new way of looking at what was said. Because of this different way of looking, and because time had passed and his own ideas had developed what the play of *After the Rain* says is more complex and more considered than what the novel says.

NOTE TO PERFORMERS

Anyone wishing to perform this play before the Lord Chamberlain's duties of censorship are abolished will have to take account of the changes he demanded before he would issue a licence.

(1) The word 'sod' occurs three times in the text, twice as a noun, once as a verb. Lord Cobbold did not object to the use of the word 'sod' as a verb, but would not allow it as a noun.

(2) The word 'bollocking' occurs twice. The Lord Chamberlain would not permit 'bollocking' or 'bullocking' and at the time of going to press the use of 'rollocking', with the 'r' clearly rolled, was under discussion with his office.

(3) 'Now that one can duplicate the Virgin Birth with a darning needle' must be changed to 'Now that any competent biologist can duplicate the Virgin Birth'.

CAST

After the Rain was first presented at the Hampstead Theatre Club on 1st September 1966, directed by Vivian Matalon, designed by Brian Currah with lighting by John B. Read. The cast was as as follows:

University Staff:

The Lecturer	ROBERT JAMES
His Two Assistants	ANDREW BRADFORD and
	GEOFFREY TODD

Prisoners Presenting:

Captain Hunter	ANTHONY OLIVER
Arthur Henderson	ALEC MCCOWEN
Gertrude Forbes-Cooper	VALERIE WHITE
Tony Batch	DOUGLAS SHELDON
Wesley Otterdale	MALCOLM ROGERS
Muriel Otterdale	MAUREEN PRYOR
Harold Banner	ALAN MACNAUGHTAN
Alan Armitage	WILLIAM MARLOWE
Sonya Banks	BARBARA YOUNG

ACT ONE

*The curtain is up. Only a few simple and necessary objects
are on what is otherwise a bare stage. There are eight
straight chairs against the back wall. There is a lectern
to one side, downstage. Also to one side, where the wings
would be, are chairs for the two* ASSISTANTS, *and a wooden
table which has a number of hand props on it—books, the
logbook,* HUNTER's *home-made spear. There are also
large white cards in holders. One card is lettered* 'HOLD',
one 'CABIN', *one* 'SALOON', *two* 'DECK', *and two* 'SEA'.
NOTE ON THE OBJECTS AND ON COSTUMES:
Two hundred years after the Rain of 1967, *a society has
grown, founded by the six survivors of our play. (There
may have been other societies from other survivors, but
we are not concerned with them.) The clothes and
furniture of this society will be based on an imperfect
tradition of what life was like in Britain in* 1967,
*modified by the fact that this society has had to rediscover
a large number of skills. Clothes and furniture should not
be outrageous or science-fictionish, but they should be
different. Prisoners should wear identical uniforms.
House lights remain up, as the* ASSISTANTS *enter and take
their places. Then the* LECTURER *enters, and arranges his
notes on the lectern. When he is ready:*

LECTURER Lower the lights, please, Mr. Porter, and take the
names of any late-comers. I'll see them in punishment
room this evening after Discussion.
(House lights lowered)
In my first lecture, I tried to give a general review of
life before the Rain of 1968. For our reconstruction of
that time we have to rely on secondary sources—that
is, on the books actually on board the raft on which our
forefathers survived. I myself am not convinced of the
value as source books either of *Rogue Herries* or

Better Sight Without Glasses. There are many areas
of life in 1968 about which we can only speculate.
For life on board the raft we have two direct sources.
The first is *The Book of Arthur*, which seems in part
to be allegorical. The second is the diary of Alan
Armitage. The raft itself was destroyed in the fire of
1998, and we have no picture of it. There seems to have
been a central structure, consisting of a main saloon,
with kitchen and bathroom, and a smaller cabin. The
deck ran all round this central structure, and contained
an entrance to the hold beneath.

The raft was not part of any survival scheme. It had
been built and launched before the Rain began by the
International Unitarian Breakfast Food Company, the
makers of Glub, a kind of cereal food. (*Clicks fingers*)
Placards, please.

(ASSISTANTS *hold up placards illustrating a packet of
Glub Flakes*)

Thank you. What you see is a box of Glub Flakes.
There were also Glub Grits, Glub Cushions, and
Poppity Glub for children. It was the contention of
the International Unitarian Breakfast Food Company
that man could live by Glub alone. They therefore
stocked a raft with it, and employed a man to sail it
round the world. Thank you, gentlemen. That man
was Captain Hunter.

(HUNTER *enters and takes up a position, stage centre*)
You are Hunter.

HUNTER Yes, I'm Hunter.

LECTURER By?

HUNTER George. I'm Hunter, by George. Actually

LECTURER Thank you. How did you get this employment?

HUNTER I was Regular Army, but they retired me. Everything
got so bloody technical, you see. Then I tried out for
keeping a pub, but the brewers wouldn't wear it.
Something to do with I.Q.—you had to draw patterns
upside down and say which words didn't fit. I got a bit
depressed actually. Then I was reading a copy of *The*

14

Director at my dentist's, and there was this advert to sail a raft round the world. Turned out all the other volunteers were nut cases or Norwegians, so they gave it to me.

LECTURER What happened?

HUNTER About living on Glub? Well, I did a lot of fishing.

LECTURER And?

HUNTER I got lost. Wireless conked out. Never knew whether I was coming or going.

LECTURER And?

HUNTER It started raining. Didn't stop. Dead calm, mind, wherever I was, but it just went on raining. Monotonous. Then one night I hit a fishing boat. Swamped it. Nobody in it but Arthur and Gertrude and Tony and a lot of dead chaps.

LECTURER So?

HUNTER Arthur took over.

LECTURER Sit down now.

(HUNTER *sits on one of the chairs at the back*)
These were Arthur Henderson, Gertrude Forbes-Cooper, and Anthony Batch. (*To* ASSISTANT) Henderson, next.

(ARTHUR *enters, and takes up position, while*)

LECTURER You may be puzzled by the name 'Henderson'. Our ancestors used the suffix 'son' in names just as we do—Clark*son*, Baker*son*, Master*son*, Farmer*son*—but what a 'Hender' was, we've not yet been able to discover. (*To* ARTHUR) You are Arthur Henderson?

ARTHUR (*slight pause*) Yes.

LECTURER Yes what?

ARTHUR I am Arthur Henderson.

LECTURER Profession?

ARTHUR Accountant.

LECTURER Vocation?

ARTHUR Leader.

LECTURER Explain.

ARTHUR When the orders came to move to camps on the high ground, I knew what would happen. Cholera. Rioting.

Food running out. I took a few who would follow me, and set out for myself.

LECTURER You chose badly. Most died.

ARTHUR I took those who would come. Two lived.

LECTURER Yes. (*To* ASSISTANTS) Forbes-Cooper and Batch.

(GERTRUDE *and* TONY *enter, and join* ARTHUR, *while*)

ARTHUR I began with two of the most necessary parts of man's nature. Miss Forbes-Cooper represented the Arts. Batch had bodily strength. Intelligence I had myself.

LECTURER You are Gertrude Forbes-Cooper.

GERTRUDE Yes.

LECTURER You are Anthony Batch.

TONY I am Tony Batch.

LECTURER Your life before?

GERTRUDE I taught Speech and Drama in the Earls Court Road. Then, as it rained and rained, I became quite isolated. The streets filled with water and the people in the basement tried to move upstairs. No proper arrangements had been made, and I couldn't have those people in the flat. Luckily I met Arthur shortly afterwards.

TONY 'What do you do?' he says. 'I'm a strong man,' I says. 'Right,' he says, 'I'll have you.'

LECTURER Thank you. Sit down.

(GERTRUDE *and* TONY *sit on chairs at the back, while*)
(*To* ARTHUR) What other people did you pick up when you had reached the raft?

ARTHUR I decided to accept anyone who came, if he were healthy and had some sort of skill. Unfortunately most of those we found were, by that time, no longer healthy. Consequently, they were left to die.

LECTURER (*to* ASSISTANTS) The Otterdales now, and Banner.

ARTHUR The Otterdales were in passable health, however. And Banner was clearly an educated man.

(WESLEY, MURIEL *and* BANNER *have entered, and taken up positions by* ARTHUR)

LECTURER You are Wesley Otterdale.

16

WESLEY Yes.

LECTURER Muriel Otterdale, his wife.

MURIEL Yes.

LECTURER Harold Banner, a priest of the Church in England.

BANNER Of. Not 'in'.

LECTURER What?

BANNER Lots of churches *in* England. Just the one *of*.

LECTURER Very good. (*To* MURIEL) You came from?

MURIEL Dudley. We came in a rowing boat with the vicar. We'd taken him in, do you see, when the rectory went under water.

LECTURER A rowing boat?

BANNER I rowed number Six in the Oxford boat.

MURIEL Mr. Banner's hands got all blistered, and he rowed and rowed. He wouldn't let me take a turn; he was that obstinate. And Wesley wouldn't. He said the Rain was a punishment, you see, and it was God's will not to row.

LECTURER Thank you. Sit down.

(*The three do so.* ARTHUR *lingers*)

ARTHUR There were two others.

LECTURER I know it. Sit down. (*As* ARTHUR *does so—to* ASSISTANTS) And I'll have the last two.

(*One* ASSISTANT *goes off.* ALAN *and* SONYA *enter*)

You are Sonya Banks.

SONYA I am Sonya Banks.

LECTURER You are Alan Armitage.

ALAN I am Alan Armitage.

LECTURER Sit.

(ASSISTANTS *return, pulling a board on wheels or rollers, which is to do duty as a rubber dinghy. It must be possible for two people to sit comfortably on it. It is left to one side of the* 'DECK' *space—as if in the sea. Meanwhile* ALAN *and* SONYA *sit down.* LECTURER *goes upstage to the row of chairs*)

When I snap my fingers, you will sleep until I order you to wake. You will sleep and hear nothing. When I say 'Wake', you will wake. Sleep now.

(LECTURER *snaps his fingers. All the performers drop into*
sleep, except ARTHUR, *who remains looking at the*
LECTURER)
You will sleep. I will snap my fingers once, and you
will sleep.
(*Snaps fingers. A long pause. Snaps fingers again.*
ARTHUR'S *head drops in sleep.* LECTURER *hesitates a*
moment, obviously worried, then comes back downstage)
New students may be unfamiliar with our procedure
at these lectures. It is most important that there should
be no distractions from the hall. Consequently I must
ask you not to cough, whisper, or indulge in love-play
of any kind. Each of these criminals is under deep
hypnosis to enable him to be the person he presents to
you. Before the Rain, this was called acting, and was
used, as we use it, for educational purposes. If the
hypnosis should be broken by distraction, the
consequences might be unfortunate. Please remember
that, although these people are criminals, that is no
reason for you to put them at risk, especially since,
when this task is over, they will have earned remission
and will be permitted to return to normal Community
Duties.
(*He speaks to the characters*)
Wake.
(*They do so*)
Places.
(ALAN *and* SONYA *enter the boat.* ARTHUR *takes his chair*
to the upstairs section, and sits. GERTRUDE, MURIEL,
WESLEY *and* BANNER *take theirs to the Main Saloon.*
HUNTER *puts on a pair of oilskins, and goes on deck.*
TONY *stays where he is*)

LECTURER Raining.
(HUNTER *turns up his collar and reacts to the rain*)
Begin.
(ALAN *and* SONYA *have also reacted to the rain, but more*
as if they had been in it for a long time, and are used to
being soaked. ALAN *is rowing. An* ASSISTANT *pulls the*

board perhaps one step forward. SONYA *is singing in a little thin voice*)

SONYA Cruising down the river,
   On a Sunday afternoon.
   The sun above, and one you love . . .

ALAN Hush up, love. I can see a light. (*Calls*) Ahoy!
   (ASSISTANT *echoes his call in a much fainter voice, and*
   HUNTER *reacts to the* ASSISTANT)

ASSISTANT Ahoy!
   (HUNTER *cocks his head and listens*)

ALAN Ahoy! Ahoy there!

ASSISTANT (*fainter*) Ahoy! Ahoy there!
   (HUNTER *turns and goes into Main Cabin, where* BANNER
   has opened one of the books on the table, and is reading.
   GERTRUDE *seems* (*in mime*) *to be knitting some intractable*
   material, WESLEY *stares straight in front of him, and*
   MURIEL *watches* WESLEY. ALAN *continues to row, and*
   ASSISTANT *takes another couple of steps forward*)

HUNTER Arthur?

BANNER Inside.
   (HUNTER *goes to upstairs section and mimes knocking*)

HUNTER Arthur?

ARTHUR Yes?

HUNTER Permission to enter, Arthur?

ARTHUR What is it?

HUNTER A shout. Somebody else must have found us.

ALAN (*calls*) Ahoy!

ASSISTANT (*not as faint as before*) Ahoy!

ARTHUR Could you see anything?

HUNTER No, Arthur. The rain . . .

ARTHUR Very well. (*Gets up*) I shall come with you. Do you have
   your spear?

HUNTER It's in the loo.

ARTHUR Get it.

HUNTER Aye, aye, Arthur.
   (*Second* ASSISTANT *comes forward, takes spear from the*
   table, and gives it to HUNTER, *while* ARTHUR *moves into*
   Main Cabin)

19

ALAN Ahoy! Ahoy there!

ASSISTANT (*nearer*) Ahoy! Ahoy there!

HUNTER Ready, Arthur?

ARTHUR Yes. Go first with your spear.

> (HUNTER *goes out on deck, followed by* ARTHUR.
> ASSISTANT *brings the wooden board almost to the edge of
> the deck space.* ALAN *stops rowing*)

ALAN Ahoy! Is anyone there?

ARTHUR Stay where you are.

> (ALAN *rows a stroke.* ASSISTANT *a little forward*)

ALAN Can we come aboard?

> (ARTHUR *motions* HUNTER *to the edge.* HUNTER *takes up
> a position of offence*)

ARTHUR Stay where you are, I said. If you come any closer, I
shall request Captain Hunter to jab you with his spear.

SONYA Goodness!

ARTHUR Are you ready, Captain Hunter?

HUNTER Aye, aye, Arthur.

ARTHUR Then stand by to repel boarders.

ALAN Is anything wrong? Can we come aboard?

SONYA He can't mean it.

ARTHUR Hunter!

> (HUNTER *appears about to jab downwards*)
> I've warned you. You have only yourselves to blame if
> you should sustain injury.
> (*A pause.* ALAN *looks at* SONYA)

ALAN Come on, Sonn. We'll be on our way.

> (*Turning motion with mimed paddle.* ASSISTANT *turns
> board*)

SONYA (*wails*) Oh, please can't we stay!

ALAN We'll find somewhere else.

> (*Board moves a little away*)

HUNTER (*uncomfortable*) Er . . . Permission to speak, Arthur?

ARTHUR Yes.

HUNTER They do look . . . harmless, you know.

ARTHUR That is not the question. (*Calls*) You! Boat people! You
need not leave us yet.

> (ALAN *stops rowing. Board turns a little back*)

I wish to interrogate you, if you are prepared to suffer it.

SONYA Oh, we are, we are.

ARTHUR Who are you? Are you husband and wife?

ALAN } No.
SONYA } Yes.

ARTHUR } What? Speak up. Answer clearly.
ALAN } Yes, we are.

SONYA Not exactly.

ARTHUR It is of no consequence. Circumstances will force us to adopt a new view of social relationships. How old is the woman?

ALAN Twenty-three.

ARTHUR Is she healthy?

SONYA I'm a bit damp.

ALAN She's healthy.

ARTHUR So I see. I suppose we could take the woman anyway. You!—What do you do?

ALAN Do?

ARTHUR For a living.

(*Pause*)

ALAN I'm a cook.

(SONYA *looks at* ALAN *in amazement.* HUNTER *grounds his spear, and speaks joyfully to* ARTHUR)

HUNTER A cook! I say, Arthur, do you think he can cook fish?

ARTHUR Can you cook fish?

ALAN I can cook anything.

HUNTER Must be all right, then?

ARTHUR There is nothing to be lost by trying him. He may be able to devise a dish which incorporates your breakfast cereal, Captain Hunter.

HUNTER Oh, I say!

ARTHUR You may allow them to board the raft. The dinghy at least may be useful to us. See if you can find some bolt or hook to which it may be secured.

HUNTER There's a sort of ring thing.

ARTHUR By all means, let them use the ring thing. Carry on, Captain Hunter.

21

HUNTER Aye, aye, Arthur.

> (ARTHUR *turns, goes into the cabin, and sits. Meanwhile,*
> HUNTER *has extended his spear, butt first, and* ALAN—
> *with the* ASSISTANT *pulling—has moved the raft close*
> *enough for* SONYA *to grasp the butt of the spear. Board*
> *is pulled right close to* 'DECK' *cards*)
> You can come up, then, eh?
> (SONYA *mimes pulling herself aboard.* HUNTER *puts down*
> *spear to help her*)

HUNTER How do you do.

SONYA How do you do.

> (ALAN *mimes climbing aboard*)

HUNTER My name's Hunter.

SONYA Yes, we heard. (*Looks around*) It's nice here.

HUNTER Oh . . . Do you think so?

SONYA Nicer than that old dinghy, I must say. Sort of palatial really.

ALAN My name's Alan Armitage. This is Sonya Banks. Do you want me to tie our dinghy up?

HUNTER No, I'll do it. The ring thing's a bit difficult to find.

ALAN Thank you.

> (HUNTER *takes the board to stage right and ties it up,*
> ASSISTANT *takes spear from him*)

SONYA Why did you tell them you were a cook? You're a writer.

ALAN He wouldn't have let me on board unless I could do something useful.

SONYA He didn't ask me.

ALAN What?

SONYA If I could . . . Anything. Just if I was healthy. *Can* you cook?

ALAN I'm not bad. (*Pause*) We can take a chance, and go. Find somewhere else. (*Pause*) I'm supposed to protect you.

SONYA You've done all right. (*Pause*) What do you think?

ALAN I think we should stay.

> (HUNTER *returns*)

HUNTER Expect you'd like to come in and meet the chaps, eh?

ALAN Yes, we should.

22

HUNTER Well, it's in here. I'll go first.

> (HUNTER *goes into the Main Cabin area.* ALAN *starts to follow.* SONYA *touches his arm. He turns, and looks at her. Then he puts his arm around her, and they kiss, passionately, as if they weren't sure when they'd have the chance again. Hold it, then*)

LECTURER Supper.

> (*They move immediately to their places.* ARTHUR *remains in the cabin.* MURIEL *is serving stew from an imaginary stewpot.* ALAN, SONYA, BANNER, GERTRUDE, HUNTER, *and* WESLEY *take their places at the table, leaving a place for* TONY, *and the head of the table empty for* ARTHUR. TONY *takes station on deck as if fishing*)

LECTURER Begin.

MURIEL I told Arthur I couldn't cook fish. Wesley doesn't like it—he's never cared for it. I said to Arthur, You can't do what you're not used to in this world, and I've never been used to cooking fish. And he said, being as there was only fish to cook, I'd have to make a start at it, but if we found anyone better, I could leave off.

HUNTER (*to* ALAN) Now we've found you, eh? Lucky thing really. No offence, Mrs. Otterdale.

ALAN Very lucky.

HUNTER Of course we all have our tasks. Discipline must be maintained, eh. Always things to be done. That's what Arthur says. When I was here on my own, I got a bit slack actually. Wrong. I see that now.

ALAN What sort of things?

BANNER Making nets. Stuffing the cracks in barrels with string.

MURIEL It's called caulking. It makes the toilet smell of glue.

HUNTER Fishing. Cooking. Look-out duty.

BANNER Sweeping out the hold. Straightening nails. Making furniture out of old crates.

GERTRUDE Reading aloud after supper. Discussion Groups.

WESLEY (*tops them: censorious*) The crackling of thorns beneath the pot!

> (*Pause*)

MURIEL Well, I'll go and call him, then.

23

(MURIEL *moves to the* 'CABIN' *area, and mimes knocking*)

ARTHUR Just coming.

ALAN What does he do in there?

BANNER I believe he thinks a great deal.

ARTHUR (*has joined them*) Where is Mr. Batch?

HUNTER Fishing.

ARTHUR No matter. We shall start without him. Mr. Banner, please say grace.

BANNER For what we are about to receive, may the Lord make us truly thankful.

ARTHUR Amen. (*To them all*) Start.
(*They mime eating*)

ALAN I'd be a bit more thankful if it were pork chops or a mixed grill.

HUNTER Or a whacking great steak. So should I, by George.

ARTHUR That will do. I don't permit irreverence, Mr. Armitage. Not for any superstitious reasons—I am an agnostic myself—but because I find that an element of formality at mealtimes helps to remind us that we are civilized beings. I should have preferred a Latin grace, but unfortunately Mr. Banner failed his degree, and cannot remember any.

BANNER I am a broad Churchman, you know.

ARTHUR On this raft, Mr. Banner, you will be the sort of churchman, *I* decide, and no other. Remember that.
(TONY *walks down the deck area, and enters the Main Cabin*)
How large is your catch?

TONY I only got three.

ARTHUR You are below your target, then.

TONY I'm sorry, Arthur. I'd have stayed out there, but what with the corpses and that in the water, you can't get them to take an interest.

ARTHUR We are at supper, Mr. Batch.

TONY Sorry.

ARTHUR You had better meet Mr. Armitage. He is to be our chef from now on. And this is Miss Banks. Mr. Batch is a strong man; Miss Banks is a dancer. I expect you

24

will have much in common.

(TONY—*a sort of half-nod, half-bow*)

SONYA A strong man?

TONY Well, I do exercises like. With weights and that.

SONYA Where?

TONY Y.M.C.A. Tottenham Court Road.

(TONY *goes off into the kitchen*)

SONYA (*disappointed*) Oh . . . I thought he meant . . .

GERTRUDE Hardly on board, my dear. There are no facilities. It is not like the care of the voice. He would require equipment of the most complicated sort.

SONYA I thought there might be a hold somewhere.

(TONY *returns*)

ARTHUR But there is a hold. That is an excellent idea. A recreational facility with an important practical value. Do you think you could improvise equipment, Mr. Batch?

TONY Equipment?

ARTHUR Weights.

TONY I could make something. With boxes and bits of chain and that. You'd have to get them balanced.

ARTHUR Excellent, excellent.

TONY Then I'd need a bit of board. For when you lie down on an inclined plane. What they call an inclined plane, in the gym. That's for lying on. And lifting. You lie on it, and then you lift. It strengthens the stomach.

ARTHUR Captain Hunter, no doubt there are bits of board in the hold?

HUNTER By George, yes. Lots of bits of board.

TONY I'd need a bit of board, then, for the inclined plane.

ARTHUR And you shall have one.

TONY Then there's press-ups. You don't need nothing for press-ups. And pull-ups, I could do.

(TONY *comes to sit down by* SONYA. *It is clear that he regards her as someone who shares his interests*)

SONYA I thought . . .

ARTHUR Yes, Miss Banks? What did you think? Have no hesitation in telling me.

25

SONYA I thought if Tony was going to practise in the hold, maybe I could too.

(*Slight pause.* ARTHUR *looks at* SONYA *and* TONY *and gets the beginnings of an idea*)

ARTHUR You wish to lift weights? I can think of no medical reason against it.

SONYA Just to do my barre, you know. If dancers don't practise, it's awfully hard to get back to it.

ALAN (*a little unhappy*) Er . . .

ARTHUR (*tops him*) By all means, Miss Banks; by all means. Our new society will need every skill, every art. (*Looks from* SONYA *to* TONY) Practise by all means. Miss Forbes-Cooper, Mrs. Otterdale, you have not finished your stew. Finish it up. We all need nourishment. Mr. Otterdale!

(MURIEL *gives* WESLEY *a nudge and he resumes eating*)

As for you, Mr. Armitage, you will be wanting to shave.

ALAN Oh, I don't know.

ARTHUR You will find a razor in the kitchen cupboard. There is no soap, but you will discover that the skin soon gets used to that.

ALAN Hunter has a beard.

ARTHUR He had it when we arrived.

HUNTER I keep it trimmed, you know.

ARTHUR Exactly, Mr. Banner!

BANNER For what we have just received may the Lord make us truly thankful.

ARTHUR Amen.

LECTURER Wait.

(*Characters remain still.* LECTURER *speaks to audience*)
The Book of Arthur is in fact a set of books. It began as the Ship's Log, and was kept up irregularly by Hunter—there are occasional entries—'Thunder today' or 'Trouble with sharks', and a number of asterisks that may have referred—oh, to some solitary sexual practices. Arthur himself began to write up the log on his arrival, but all the early material has been amended, crossed out, and written over. For a

26

statement of Arthur's intentions at the beginning of the voyage, the Diary of Alan Armitage appears to be a more reliable source. (*To* CHARACTERS) Conversation on deck.

(ALAN *and* ARTHUR *leave their places at the table, and begin to pace the deck*)

ARTHUR Tell me, Mr. Armitage, have you come to any explanation in your mind about this flood?

ALAN God, I suppose.

ARTHUR So Mr. Otterdale would say. He believes it to be some form of divine punishment for his own sins. A common delusion.

ALAN Has he sinned much?

ARTHUR Hardly at all.

ALAN Potty?

ARTHUR One might say so.

ALAN I'm surprised you keep him.

(*Pause.* ARTHUR *looks sharply at* ALAN)

ARTHUR His wife is attached to him.

ALAN And Mr. Banner? Doesn't *he* say God's sent the rain?

ARTHUR Mr. Banner is a very broad Churchman. It is not clear that he believes in God at all.

ALAN And you?

ARTHUR I say that it is the best thing that could ever have happened.

ALAN I don't understand you.

ARTHUR I do a lot of reading in my spare time. I have been practising the strictest mental discipline ever since I was a boy. If I had not done so, I should not be in command here, and if I were not in command, it is doubtful whether any of you would survive.

ALAN You think we shall, then?

ARTHUR I have no doubt of it. Natural Selection is responsible for this rain, and by Natural Selection certain people will survive it. I shall be one of them. So will you, as long as you obey me.

ALAN Why did Natural Selection pick us, do you think?

ARTHUR I can see you are not a serious student of human

27

affairs, Mr. Armitage.

ALAN So much of my life has been spent in the kitchen.

ARTHUR Then let me use a kitchen metaphor to explain matters to you. What happens when you have too many bottles of milk, too many tomatoes?

ALAN They go bad.

ARTHUR Exactly. And that is what has happened to the human race.

ALAN Too many people?

ARTHUR Far too many. And they have been increasing at an increasing rate. People have spawned people.

ALAN Yes. They do that.

ARTHUR And not only were men increasing their numbers, so that in three generations we should have used up the natural resources of the world, but worse—far worse—the poorer, more brutish sort were increasing faster than the rest. Have you any idea of the rise in the rate of mental deficiency in Great Britain over the past thirty years?

ALAN Er——

ARTHUR No, of course you haven't. But I have. I read. I can see things. I am not blind, like some.

ALAN No, indeed.

ARTHUR The proportion of morons and near-morons has been a rising curve, Mr. Armitage, because although one can persuade intelligent people to control their numbers, one cannot teach contraception to idiots. Idiots have more and more outnumbered the intelligent and, under a system of democracy, had as much political power. Lunacy! The rain has wiped that out. Only intelligent people will survive it, and such of the less intelligent as they choose to carry with them.

ALAN Why carry any?

ARTHUR For the rough work.

ALAN What if they refuse?

ARTHUR They won't refuse. Does Mr. Batch refuse? Does Captain Hunter?

ALAN No.

28

ARTHUR Do you refuse?

    (*Pause*)

ALAN No.

ARTHUR You know when you're well off. So do they. There
will be much for everyone to do when the waters
subside, and we begin our settlement. And with careful
breeding, inherited characteristics——

ALAN Breeding?

    (*Pause*)

ARTHUR We should have to match the children very carefully,
should we not?

ALAN Oh.

ARTHUR We are a small group.

ALAN If you're so keen on children, why do we sleep with the
men and women separated?

ARTHUR Oh, there will be time for that, Mr. Armitage. And I
do not intend, you know, to enforce a total chastity.
There must be many occasions when you and Miss
Banks can . . .

ALAN We're never alone together. You know that.

ARTHUR Surely you could make the opportunity. She spends
a good deal of time alone in the hold with Mr. Batch
as it is. They do their exercises together.

    (*Pause*)

ALAN What if the waters never do subside?

ARTHUR They will. Do you imagine that Natural Selection
intends to replace us by fish?

    (*Pause*)

LECTURER Exercises in the hold.

    (ALAN *and* ARTHUR *return to their seats.* TONY *and*
SONYA *come into the* 'HOLD' *area*)

    Begin.

    (TONY *mimes his weight-lifting exercises.* SONYA *does her
barre, counting to herself,* 'One an' two an' three an' four
an' . . .')

SONYA There was a boy I knew ruptured himself lifting
heavy weights.

TONY There's right and wrong ways of doing anything.

    29

SONYA Well, he was a bit simple. He left the show at
Portsmouth. Went off with a sailor. He said he'd
promised his mum he'd never marry unless it was int
the navy.

TONY I saw some ballet once.

SONYA (*pleased*) Did you?

TONY It was on the telly. There was this geezer with long
sleeves and a dirty great bow tie. And a lot of birds i
white skirts.

SONYA Birds?

TONY Girls.

SONYA Oh . . . I thought you meant 'Swan Lake'.

TONY Must be good for your muscles, all that, then?

SONYA Mmm.

TONY Sort of like what I do. Only it develops you in differer
places. Like with us it's the chest and arms more. An
with you it's the legs.

SONYA (*counting*) One an' two an' three an' . . .

TONY Sort of artistic really. I done some artistic poses once
for a photographer. Showing off me pectorals. I had t
rub this oil all over me. Then it got on the sheets afte

SONYA We don't do that.

TONY That what you're doing now—do you do that in show
like?

SONYA No. I do modern.

TONY (*not understanding*) Oh, yes?

SONYA Do you want to see? Here, you count for me.

TONY Count?

SONYA Like I was doing. One an' two an' three an'——

TONY (*begins laboriously*) One an' two an'——

SONYA Only do it with a syncopated beat. A one and a two
and a three and a four. And clap, eh? Like this.
(SONYA *shows him a quick, syncopated beat, clapping h
hands. As he begins, she goes into a modern routine. He
gets faster and faster. She can't keep up, and starts to
laugh.* ALAN *leaves his seat, and begins to walk slowly
towards the* HOLD *area.* TONY *begins to laugh also. Th
routine and clapping break down, as they are both laughin*

30

(ALAN *comes into the* HOLD)

ALAN What's the joke?

SONYA It's Tony. He can't count.

TONY I can, then. She can't keep up.

ALAN Sorry to interrupt. I just thought I'd see how you were
getting on.

(LECTURER *speaks. The characters remain still*)

LECTURER (*to* AUDIENCE) Armitage's diary is not a wholly reliable
source. One has to consider that any diarist is likely to
be a self-centred person, who exaggerates his own
importance. Armitage believed, first that Arthur
considered him as a possible rival, second that Arthur
deliberately encouraged an association between Miss
Banks and Tony Batch so as to cripple Armitage with
jealousy. If there was really a contest for leadership, it
was over a trivial matter, and Armitage lost. (*To
characters*) Places for the evening discussion. Book
Cricket.

(WESLEY *goes on deck as a look-out.* BANNER *and*
HUNTER *begin a game of book-cricket at the table,
watched by* MURIEL. TONY *and* SONYA *remain in the
Hold.* ARTHUR *goes to the cabin,* GERTRUDE *to the
kitchen, where she will mime trying to shred a twig,
watched by* ALAN)

BANNER Oh dear! Poor Kenneth Barrington has been bowled.

HUNTER Luck of the game, old man. Bowled Trueman—seven.

BANNER I don't know why you keep Trueman on. You'd think
he'd be tired by now.

HUNTER Just bowled Barrington, didn't he?

(ALAN *has come in from the kitchen, and is picking over
the books*)

ALAN I hope you're not using *Jamaica Inn* for your book
cricket, because I'm reading it.

BANNER (*looking*) No, it's *Principles of Navigation Under Sail.*

HUNTER Where's old Gertrude?

ALAN Making toothbrushes. She says the natives of India
use shredded twigs, and have the whitest teeth in the
world. She got it from the *Children's Encyclopaedia.*

31

HUNTER I brought that. It's not one of the Company's books.
  (ALAN *has found 'Jamaica Inn'*)

MURIEL You'll not have much time for your reading. It's nearly time for Study Period.

BANNER What is it tonight?

ALAN Shakespeare.
  (GERTRUDE *has come in from the kitchen.* ARTHUR *leaves the cabin and joins them, at first unobserved*)

GERTRUDE Can I be doing it wrong? The twigs won't shred. All that happens when I clean my teeth is that I get a mouthful of bark.

ARTHUR You need a special sort of wood, Miss Forbes-Cooper. You should have read further into the encyclopaedia.

MURIEL Arthur knows. Arthur always knows.

GERTRUDE Arthur, how foolish of me! I am truly sorry.

ARTHUR No, no, Miss Forbes-Cooper. We learn by doing. Where are the others?

MURIEL Wesley's doing Look-out. It's his task.

ARTHUR (*smiles*) And no doubt Mr. Batch and Miss Banks are . . . practising together?

HUNTER Always at it.

MURIEL Yes, they are.

ALAN What do you mean by that?

HUNTER Always at it. Exercises. I thought I might do it.

ALAN Then why don't you?

HUNTER Two's company.

MURIEL That's right.

ALAN I think you should be careful what you're saying.

HUNTER Don't see *you* down there, by George.

ALAN I do the cooking. You know that.

HUNTER There you are, then.

ALAN If you want to do exercises, then do them. Don't hang around hinting.

HUNTER Who's hinting? I'm not hinting.

ALAN They'd be glad to have you, if you want to know. I was down there myself. They asked me. I watched for a bit, and came back. Any one of us can go down at any time. Watch, join in, or anything. So you can keep

32

your insinuations, and stuff them. Right?

ARTHUR I agree. Captain Hunter, you will not upset Mr. Armitage. He is too busy with the cooking to make frequent trips to see what goes on in the hold, but he is glad, as we all are, that Miss Banks has found a friend. Meanwhile, please call them, Miss Forbes-Cooper. I wish to hold a conference on a minor matter. (GERTRUDE *goes to where the door is imagined to be, opens it, but keeps out of the wet. She calls*)

GERTRUDE Sonya! Tony! Arthur wants you.

MURIEL Wesley!

ARTHUR (*to* WESLEY) Make your report, Mr. Otterdale.

WESLEY My eyes have seen nothing.

ARTHUR Then sit down, everybody, and attend.
(*They compose themselves roughly as an audience, though there must be room for chairs to be moved, as will appear*)

ARTHUR I have been considering the problem of damp. Who here has any ideas to contribute on that subject?
(*Pause. They look at each other*)

MURIEL Wesley's got foot rot. I haven't liked to say. And it's not healthy, never having dry underwear.

ARTHUR The problem is solved. We shall light the stove one day a week.

SONYA Oh, bliss!

ARTHUR We shall use some of the wooden crates in the hold to start the fire. Perhaps Glub itself will burn. Then we shall stack wet driftwood against the stove to dry, when it will be burned in its turn, and dry other driftwood.

GERTRUDE Dear Arthur! At all times so far-seeing!

ARTHUR The thought came to me this afternoon.

HUNTER That's old Arthur's task, by George. Thinking, that's *his* task. Does it all the time, too. No rest periods.

ALAN Well, we can all think I hope.

HUNTER Not our task, though, is it?

ALAN There's plenty of driftwood. We can have the stove going all the time once it's started. Stupid just to do it once a week.

ARTHUR You find my arrangements stupid, Mr. Armitage?

ALAN Well, it's not really an arrangement yet, is it? I mean, we're still discussing it.

ARTHUR No. *You* are still discussing it.

(*Silence.* GERTRUDE *moves away from* ALAN)

ALAN Dammit, we can discuss it, Arthur. Kick it around a bit.

MURIEL Excuse me.

(MURIEL *moves*)

ALAN Arthur, I'm not opposing you or anything. All I'm saying is that we can quite easily——

ARTHUR I'm delighted to find that Mr. Armitage considers himself equally able to take decisions. It is a quality of leadership.

(BANNER *also moves*)

BANNER (*nervous*) We don't disagree with Arthur here.

HUNTER By George, no. Better not, eh?

MURIEL Arthur knows what's good for us.

(SONYA *comes and stands beside* ALAN. TONY *does not appear to notice what is happening.* ALAN *looks at* SONYA *and then at* ARTHUR)

ARTHUR Pray do not distress yourself, Miss Banks. Mr. Armitage knows where his duty lies.

ALAN What duty?

ARTHUR To yourself. To us all. To Miss Banks, certainly. On board ship, a mutineer puts his close friends in danger.

ALAN Perhaps I was wrong.

ARTHUR Are you sorry for that?

ALAN Yes, I am sorry.

ARTHUR It would be improvident—do you agree?—to burn *all* the wood.

ALAN It was a very stupid suggestion. I see that now.

ARTHUR Nevertheless you may feel free to *make* suggestions, Mr. Armitage. I shall decide whether they be stupid or not.

ALAN Thank you, Arthur.

ARTHUR Ladies, and gentlemen, pray resume your former places. There is plenty of room near Mr. Armitage.

(*All return to their former positions, while*)

34

And now, Miss Forbes-Cooper, if you would care to proceed with the Study Period?

GERTRUDE We were doing *Julius Caesar*.

ARTHUR Caesar was a great man. He found his vocation, as I have, in middle life. (*Leaving*) Proceed, Miss Forbes-Cooper.

(GERTRUDE *comes to the front of the class* ARTHUR *to cabin*)

GERTRUDE (*coughs importantly*) Would anyone like to tell me where we left off on Monday?

BANNER We were discussing the murder of Caesar as myth, as I remember.

SONYA You said they'd all killed their father.

GERTRUDE Quite right, my dear. Caesar was a father to the Romans, and when the conspirators killed him, all the people shared in their triumph and their guilt. Because as Freud tells us, everybody wants to kill his father.

HUNTER Oh, I say!

GERTRUDE Hero worship is followed by the destruction of heroes.

BANNER That's very true.

GERTRUDE That destruction may give joy, but it will also cause guilt, and it is upon this guilt that Antony plays. Is that clear?

BANNER Most clear and interesting.

MURIEL Oh, yes. Very.

GERTRUDE Mr. Batch?

(TONY's *attention has obviously wandered*)

SONYA You shouldn't go so fast for him.

GERTRUDE I cannot adjust the pace of the class to its slowest member.

SONYA (*to* TONY) She says that when they killed Caesar they were killing someone who was like a father to them.

TONY Yeah . . . Well, that's wrong, ennit?

GERTRUDE It is not wrong, Mr. Batch. It is part of the natural order.

TONY Like Arthur—you take Arthur. I mean, he's in charge; he's the gaffer. That don't mean it's right to——

WESLEY The fool hath said in his heart—There is no God.

35

Corrupt are they, and have done abominable iniquity.
There is none that doeth good.

(WESLEY *begins to make a droning noise*)

BANNER Perhaps you had better remind us of Antony's speech,
Gertrude. Then we should have it fresh in our
memories.

WESLEY Every one of them is gone back. They are altogether
become filthy.

GERTRUDE Come now, Harold. Surely that isn't necessary.

WESLEY There is none that doeth good, no not one.

BANNER You do it so well. We should all profit by it.

WESLEY The workers of iniquity eat up all my people as they
eat bread.

MURIEL Give over now, Wesley. Gertrude's going to speak
some poetry. You'll like that.

GERTRUDE Well . . . perhaps just the beginning. I shall have to
stand on something. And you can all be citizens.

(BANNER *and* HUNTER *help her on to the table. Her
audience stands round. She begins to declaim*)

Friends, Romans, Countrymen, lend me your ears. I
come to bury Caesar, not——

LECTURER Enough.

(*Pause.* GERTRUDE *deflated*)

GERTRUDE What?

LECTURER Thank you. Enough.

(BANNER *and* HUNTER *help* GERTRUDE *down again.
Hold the silence long enough to communicate a feeling of
hurt and resentment from* GERTRUDE. *They take their
places in the Main Saloon, sitting in silence. Meanwhile*)

LECTURER Mr. Armitage, the storm, please. From the beginning.

(ALAN *takes a chair from the Saloon, brings it out on
deck. Begins to mime fishing. Meanwhile*)

As I explained in my first lecture, we do not know
exactly when the rain began, because nobody noticed
it. They only began to take notice, when it did not stop.
In its nature, it appears to have been a calm, settled
downpour, with no wind. On 26th June 1970, when the
rain had continued for approximately two years this

calm was broken.

(ALAN *moves on his chair, as if the raft should be beginning to rock a little. When he notices what is happening, he is surprised. He gets up, and begins to go indoors. All look up as* ALAN *goes swiftly through the Main Cabin and into the upstairs area*)

HUNTER What's up?

(*No reply.* ALAN *mimes knocking*)

ARTHUR Yes?

ALAN Permission to speak, Arthur?

ARTHUR Yes.

ALAN Something's up. There's a sort of swell beginning. And there's a wind coming up.

ARTHUR Well?

ALAN It's been dead calm for months.

ARTHUR Yes.

(*As if the whole raft rocks violently. All react to this*)
There is some motion, certainly.

(*He gets up, and comes into the Main Cabin*)

GERTRUDE Arthur——

ARTHUR I am going outside to see.

(WESLEY *begins the same droning noise we have heard before*)
Belay that, Mr. Otterdale.

(ALAN *and* ARTHUR *go on deck*)

ALAN It's got much darker.

ARTHUR Yes.

(*Another lurching motion. All react.* ARTHUR *goes back as if to call through into the Main Cabin*)
A distinct motion. Most distinct. Captain Hunter, come outside please.

(HUNTER *has begun to get into his oilskins, while*)

SONYA What's happening?

HUNTER Looks as if we're in for a bit of a blow.

(*He goes out on deck*)
Looks as if——

ARTHUR What action do you usually take under these circumstances?

HUNTER Get the sail down.

ARTHUR Yes. Mr. Batch will help you.

(ALAN *goes to door of Main Cabin, and calls*)

ALAN Tony!

(TONY *gets up*)

ARTHUR Mr. Armitage and Mr. Otterdale will bring the rubber dinghy indoors. I should not care to lose it.

ALAN (*calls*) And Wesley!

(*Nudged by* MURIEL, WESLEY *joins* TONY)

ARTHUR And after the sail?

HUNTER I go inside, shut the door, pull that sort of shutter thing across it so the cabin doesn't get flooded, and go to sleep.

(*Another violent rocking.* GERTRUDE *falls over on* MURIEL. TONY *and* WESLEY, *after it, stagger out on deck*)

MURIEL (*a howl*)

TONY Muriel's cut her lip. That Gertrude fell on her.

ARTHUR No time for that. Captain Hunter, let us begin.

HUNTER Aye, aye, Arthur. We've got to take the sail down, old Tone.

ARTHUR Mr. Armitage——

(HUNTER *and* TONY *have begun to move, but* HUNTER *sees something*)

HUNTER Christ!

ARTHUR What?

HUNTER (*shouts*) Hang on! Hang on to something!

(*All dive for what is solid and nearest*)

Bloody tidal wave.

(*Violent reactions as wave hits.* BANNER *and women clinging to table in cabin*)

LECTURER Wait!

(*All freeze*)

It seems that there was a succession of monstrous waves. The raft would tilt as they were carried up to the crest. There the wind would hit them. Then they would slide down into a trough again—where they were at least sheltered from the wind. (*To* ASSISTANTS) Wind this time. (*To Cast*) Continue!

38

(ASSISTANT *leaves stage. From now on, wind heard when a wave hits them, diminishing in volume when they are comparatively at rest, in the trough of a wave.* WESLEY *drones when not speaking*)

ARTHUR The dinghy, Mr. Armitage.

ALAN Come on, Wesley.

WESLEY The Lord is mighty in anger. He sendeth the storm to chastise us.

HUNTER Come on, old Tone. Get cracking, eh? (*Sees wave approaching*) No! Wait!

ALAN Wesley, hang on.
(*Wave hits. When they recover*)

HUNTER Right?
(WESLEY *moves forward to the centre of the deck*)

WESLEY Oh Lord, we are fit and ready for thy chastisement.

ARTHUR Get him back.
(ALAN *gets him back*)

WESLEY (*struggles against* ALAN's *hold*) We are thy servants, oh Lord, thy slaves and chattels. Not as we will, but as thou wilt, oh Lord.

HUNTER Wave!
(TONY *dives for what he has been holding on to.* WESLEY *pulls away*)

ALAN (*shouts above wind*) Hold on! Hold on, sod you!
(WESLEY *begins to cry out, without words, in a loud voice. He pulls against* ALAN, *who lets go. He is blown across the deck and into the sea. He goes limp. Wave passes*)

ARTHUR What happened?

ALAN I was holding him.

TONY He's gone now.

ALAN I may have let go.

ARTHUR Get the dinghy inside. I shall help you. Captain Hunter, Mr. Batch, you may use a knife for the sail since time is short. Instruct Mr. Banner to pray for succour, if he should not already be doing so.
(TONY *and* HUNTER *get inside to cross the saloon to reach the mast on the other side of the deck.* ARTHUR *runs quickly across to* ALAN. *A wave hits. Recovery*)

ALAN He went mad, I think.

TONY (*to* BANNER) He says you got to pray.

ARTHUR It is of no consequence. He was mad before.

BANNER What does he wish me to say?

TONY For succour, he says.

ARTHUR He was expendable.

HUNTER Come *on*, Tone.

(TONY *and* HUNTER *out on deck to rear.* ALAN *and* ARTHUR *have been working at the dinghy*)

ALAN Hold on!

(*A wave hits.* TONY *and* HUNTER *grab mast, and hold on. Recovery*)

HUNTER Quick!

(*Slash at lower rope. Then on the other's shoulders for upper. While*)

BANNER Oh Lord, if it be indeed thy design, as some have suggested, to punish us in this way for our misdeeds, be not too outrageous in thy wrath. Spare, oh Lord, the helpless. Bring succour to the distressed.

HUNTER Tone! Hurry!

(TONY *casts a scared glance at the waves, makes a slash at the rope, then drops down to deck, clinging to the mast. A wave strikes. Then recovery. The* ALAN *and* ARTHUR *get the dinghy on deck. While*)

BANNER Consider, oh Lord, that not all have been guilty in equal measure. Consider especially the women and children. Consider——

(ASSISTANT *hits* BANNER *with a book. He falls.* ARTHUR *and* ALAN *into saloon*)

ARTHUR Inside. (*They get indoors*) Shutter.

(TONY, ALAN *and* HUNTER *pull across the imaginary shutter and lock it, while*)

Why is Mr. Banner not praying?

SONYA Book hit him.

ARTHUR Porthole. (HUNTER *to porthole*) Then find something solid, and cling on.

GERTRUDE But what of Harold?

ARTHUR Hold him. It will do him no good to be flying about.

40

(*Lights down as ports closed. A wave hits. Then silence*)

MURIEL What have you done with my husband? (*Pause*) What have you done with my husband?

LECTURER (*gently*) No more now.

(LECTURER *moves across to the* CHARACTERS)

(*Still gently*) Sleep now. Rest now. No more rain now.

(ASSISTANTS *revive characters—who respond like automata—and point the way offstage. They go.*

LECTURER *returns to his place and speaks directly to the* AUDIENCE)

LECTURER Please break for ten minutes and reassemble here.

END OF ACT ONE

ACT TWO

During the interval, the cards are rearranged so as to allow a larger deck area. The characters are brought in, and sit against the back wall.

House lights lowered. LECTURER *enters. He surveys the characters, then sends them to sleep by clicking his fingers. He turns to address the audience.*

LECTURER Nobody in this hall has committed a criminal offence, or you would not of course be here. Consequently you may not realize that what you witness is not only a history lecture, but also a necessary part of the reconditioning of some unhappy people who have committed crimes against the Community. In each case, the criminal's offence has a parallel in the conduct of the historical person he is presenting. Thus your Arthur Henderson has been guilty of persistently individualistic behaviour. Your Alan Armitage has a history of petty crime—lack of group effort, public sarcasm, psycho-somatic asthma. Both your Captain Hunter and your Sonya Banks have been guilty of private pleasure and irrational enjoyment, leading to the neglect

41

of tasks. Your Gertrude Forbes-Cooper is a persistent liar, your Muriel Otterdale a murderess, your Tony Batch has been either late for or absent from Community Meetings ever since he was old enough to attend, and your Harold Banner suffers from doubt, amounting often to despair. In volunteering to present these characters, the criminals concerned are able to act out their own anti-communal tendencies, providing not only instruction for you, but therapy for themselves. (*To the* CAST) Wake! (*They do so*)

(*To* AUDIENCE) Now the sun shone, and the air was still. The raft lay becalmed. The sail hung from the mast like old washing. Since the raft did not move, the batteries which provided light and heat were not recharged. (*To* CHARACTERS) Days in the sun. The Beginning Time.

(*All but* ARTHUR *and* MURIEL *leave their chairs, walk out on to the deck area, stretch their arms, enjoy the sun. The men take off their shirts. They dispose themselves for sunbathing. While*)

(*To* AUDIENCE) They had the sun—what did they want with light and heat? Except that the sun by itself would not distil fresh water from salt, and give them water for drinking.

(ARTHUR *comes briskly out on deck, followed by* MURIEL, *who brings a chair and the log-book with her.* ARTHUR *claps his hands*)

ARTHUR I have decided to call the first meeting of the new society. (*To* MURIEL) Thank you, Mrs. Otterdale. Set it there, if you please. (*She sets chair for him*) Have you the Log-Book? Sit down. (*She does so; he continues*) This will be our Minute Book. I shall now enter the Minutes of our First Meeting. By this means, we shall have a record of our Society from the beginning. (*He sits, produces a pencil, and begins to write*) Minutes of the First Meeting of the New Society. 13th July 1969. Present . . . (*Continues to write*)

ALAN But we've no seed. No livestock. How can we survive?

ARTHUR (*while writing*) There will be a time for questions later, Mr. Armitage. Meanwhile I have not yet declared the meeting open. (*Finishes*) The meeting is open. I propose that the Society be called The New Society. All in favour?

(*All raise their hands*)

BANNER Aye.

ARTHUR Good. (*Writing*) Officers. We should not, in my view, burden ourselves with too many at first. One officer, to be called the President, and to combine the duties of President, Secretary and Treasurer, should suffice. That is my proposal. All in favour?

(*All raise their hands*)

HUNTER Aye, aye.

BANNER (*hesitantly*) I should like to propose Arthur for President.

ARTHUR Who seconds?

(*Looks at* ALAN. *Pause.*)

ALAN I do.

ARTHUR All in favour?

(*All raise their hands*

ARTHUR (*writing*) Nemine contra dicente. Next . . .

ALAN Do you think there should be any provision for a Deputy President?

ARTHUR Why?

ALAN In case anything were to happen to you, Mr. President.

ARTHUR Nothing will. Now. . . . . Rules. As your President, I shall promulgate rules from time to time. Rule One. Doubt is an infection. It can disable us. If we should discover it, we must kill it, as we should kill a virus.

ALAN Ah!

ARTHUR You spoke?

ALAN Just breathing.

ARTHUR Breathe more quietly. Any part of the body politic which doubts its survival will be cut out. Any questions.

ALAN None.

ARTHUR Rule Two. While we remain becalmed, we shall cut down on the use of power. No lights will be used. We

43

shall rise with the sun, and retire with it.

SONYA I don't mind. I can't keep up with all that Shakespeare.

ARTHUR Your minding is not in question, Miss Banks. It will be done. Furthermore, there will be no cooking. Heat will be used only to distil water.

HUNTER No stew. Just eat Glub?

ARTHUR We shall do better with fish. Only we must make shift with *au bleu.*

BANNER Blue?

ARTHUR Raw.

HUNTER Eat raw fish?

ARTHUR It is not unknown.

BANNER I suppose . . . it might be almost Japanese.

ARTHUR Exactly. A great delicacy—properly regarded. And seaweed also.

(*A buzz of appalled conversation from the others*)
Settle down. Lastly——

LECTURER Wait. (*To* AUDIENCE) The new rule was put into effect that night. (*To* CAST) Fish supper.
(*Places for supper*)

ARTHUR Mr. Banner, please ask a blessing.

BANNER (*doleful*) For what we are about to receive may the Lord make us truly thankful.

ARTHUR Amen.

(*A pause. All look at* ARTHUR. *He tastes the fish*)

ARTHUR It is unpleasant on the whole.

(HUNTER *and* BANNER *taste*)

BANNER The Japanese——

HUNTER There's always been something fishy about the Japanese.

(ALAN, TONY, MURIEL *and* GERTRUDE *taste and swallow.* SONYA *does not. All look at her*)

ARTHUR Come now, Miss Banks.

(SONYA *lifts a spoonful towards her mouth, pauses, then puts it back on the plate*)

SONYA I don't fancy it.

ARTHUR It will do you good.

SONYA Not if I bring it all up again, it won't.

ARTHUR You must keep it down.

SONYA I can't. I don't want any. Anybody can have mine.

ARTHUR (*looking around*) There is no need for us all to stop eating, just because Miss Banks is having a little difficulty with her fish.
(*They begin eating again*)

ARTHUR Now, Miss Banks, we must eat our fish. Let us try again.

MURIEL Must eat our nice fish.

GERTRUDE Yes, indeed. Delicious.

ALAN I don't see why she should be forced to eat. It's her own funeral.

ARTHUR While she is in my charge, I do not intend her funeral to take place.

ALAN Couldn't she have——

ARTHUR There will be no exceptions.

ALAN Sorry.

ARTHUR Sorrow by itself means nothing, unless it is accompanied by the intention of amendment. Do not interfere again.
(*To* SONYA, *blazing out*) Eat your fish!
(*Shocked silence. Then all but* SONYA *and* TONY (*who is eating normally*) *begin to eat at double time.* SONYA *lifts a spoonful towards her mouth again*)

ARTHUR Come now, Miss Banks. I understand your feelings. The fish is indeed nauseous at first taste. If you wish, I shall ask Mrs. Otterdale to hold your nose while you eat.

MURIEL (*delighted, begins to rise*) Hold her nose, and down it goes.
(ARTHUR *waves her down again*)

ARTHUR We shall avoid it if we can.

TONY (*gently*) Come on then, old Sonn, eh?
(*Her spoon follows his in time. She takes a mouthful, chews, swallows*)

ARTHUR Excellent, excellent! Now, all together. With me. Begin.
(*All begin eating, in time with* ARTHUR)

LECTURER Enough! (ALL *stop*) Go on to the morning of August 3rd.
(*They begin to take up places.* GERTRUDE *and* HAROLD

45

arrange a couple of chairs as back-rests for sunbathing on
deck. HUNTER *takes his spear, and begins a patrol up and*
down one side of the deck. ALAN *goes into the kitchen,*
ARTHUR *upstairs;* MURIEL *remains at the table.* TONY
and SONYA *go to the Hold, and begin their exercises.*
While)
You begin to reveal yourselves a little.

BANNER It is true I had no vocation, but I thought I might do some good in the world.

GERTRUDE I never married, you know. Nobody lasted long enough for me.

BANNER I wanted to be of use.

GERTRUDE Sir Charles Cochran once told me I was too intense for life. Born for the theatre, not for life, he said. But then he had to be polite, because he was turning me down for a part.

BANNER I wanted to help people.

GERTRUDE What? What, Harold?

BANNER I wanted to help.

GERTRUDE Why didn't you become a social worker?

BANNER The qualifications.

GERTRUDE A free hand, an open heart—surely that is all one needs?

BANNER And a degree in Social Science.

(ALAN *leaves the kitchen and moves to the hold*)
I left Oxford without a degree of any kind, so there was nothing for it but the Church.

(ALAN *stands at the entrance to the hold, and watches*
TONY *and* SONYA, *who see him almost at once, and stop*
what they are doing)

ALAN Here you are, then.

SONYA Yes.

ALAN Busy?

SONYA Not really.

ALAN I thought I might do it for a bit.

SONYA You want to do weight-lifting?

ALAN It's good for you, isn't it?

(*Pause.* TONY *and* SONYA *exchange an uncomfortable*
glance)

46

TONY You don't want to do too much at first, you know.

ALAN No?

TONY Could do yourself a damage. Hernia or something. I mean, it's been known.

ALAN I'll do something simple, then.

TONY You could try press-ups, I suppose.

ALAN All right. I'll try press-ups.

(*Pause.* TONY *motions him to get into position, and* ALAN *does so. Meanwhile* MURIEL *leaves her place at the table, and waits outside* ARTHUR's *door. While*)

BANNER You might say I drifted into it—an apt enough metaphor for a rowing man. I was given my Blue in my second year. Nobody had taken much notice of me up to then, but the Moral Rearmament people were keen to recruit athletic personalities. They asked me to tea at St. Peter's Hall. There was a Rugger Blue and a Boxing Blue and two South Africans and a peer. We had strawberries and cream, and confessed our sins.

TONY Get your arms right. They're not right.

GERTRUDE But the belief? Dogma? The matter of faith?

BANNER Oh, there's a very wide latitude of belief in the Church of England nowadays. The important thing was to do good. And really you know, I was so busy with the Youth Club, and the Suicide Service, and Meals on Wheels, and pensioners' evenings, I had little time to think about religious questions.

TONY Now—keep your back straight. Don't bend your back.

BANNER And when I did, I discovered that most things could be explained quite simply. All those doubts people used to have in Victorian novels. There was never any need for them now that one can duplicate The Virgin Birth with a darning needle, and people are being raised from the dead every day. In any case, nobody wanted me to believe in God as a person, or in Christ as anything else. Nowadays, Heaven is not a place, you know, but a oneness with God. The individual soul just dissolves into the God soul. Not an easy thing to explain to my parishioners, but then I didn't have to,

47

because they never came to church.

(MURIEL *mimes knocking*)

ARTHUR What do you want, Mrs. Otterdale?

MURIEL Just to tell you.

ARTHUR What?

MURIEL I'd always do anything *you* wanted, Arthur. You've only to ask.

ARTHUR I know it. Thank you, Mrs. Otterdale.

(ALAN *has been lying in position, occasionally lifting himself a little way, but not completing a press-up*)

TONY Come on, then.

(*Another attempt. Then* ALAN *gets out of position, and sits up*)

ALAN I can't do it.

TONY You can do *one*.

ALAN (*near tears*) I can't do one bloody press-up.

HUNTER (*shouts*) Land ho!

(HUNTER *has seen something in the distance, downstage, on the* LECTURER's *side of the stage. As the others react to his cry, the* LECTURER *stops them*)

LECTURER Wait! Boarding Party, remain: places, the rest. (*To* AUDIENCE) Armitage's diary reports that they had seen an ark. (*To* ASSISTANT) Placard, please.

(ASSISTANT *holds up placard showing a toy Noah's ark*) It is not clear what an ark was. The *Children's Encyclopaedia* appears to suggest that it was at once a kind of boat, a religious object, and a toy for children. It was filled with live animals, and carried before the people of Palestine in battle. It looked like this. (*To* ASSISTANT) Thank you. (*Placard down: to* AUDIENCE) There was a man aboard the ark. We know little about him—certainly not enough to create a personality. Consequently he will be presented to you by the university staff. (*To* ALAN *and* ARTHUR) You have boarded the ark. You smell the stench of it.

ARTHUR Something has died. And not recently. Good.

ALAN Good?

ARTHUR Whatever has died has not been cleared away. Perhaps

48

that is because there is nobody to clear it.

LECTURER There is somebody. An old man appears. (ASSISTANT
forward) His eyes are red in a face encrusted with filth
and set in a frame of matted hair. Catch him before he
falls. (*They do so*) His mouth opens, but he is parched,
and cannot speak.

ARTHUR Give him water.

(ALAN, *supports* ASSISTANT *gently, and helps him to
drink*)

Who is aboard your ark, old man?

(LECTURER *answers for the old man, but does not act.
His voice is flat, as if reading a report*)

LECTURER Dead. All dead.

ARTHUR Did you have livestock? Cows? Pigs? Chickens even?

LECTURER All dead. There was no water. And they had fouled
their quarters.

ARTHUR You had better take a look round, Mr. Armitage.

(ALAN *ceases to support the* ASSISTANT)

LECTURER I have drunk blood. Blood. I have drunk blood.

ARTHUR See if you can find anything that may be of use.

(ALAN *summons his resolution, and goes quickly through
the imaginary door to the extreme side of the stage*)

LECTURER Ham. . . . Shem. . . . Both dead. My wife left me, you
know, before the word was fulfilled. Forty days and
forty nights, I lost count. She took Japhet and went to
her married sister in Ruislip. More has occurred than
was foretold.

ARTHUR (*calls*) What do you find, Mr. Armitage?

ALAN (*returns*) Animals all dead. Sacks of grain rotting. But
there's some seed in bins.

ARTHUR In what condition?

ALAN I opened one. Looks all right.

ARTHUR Can we take them?

ALAN Too big. Sink the dinghy.

ARTHUR (*thinks*) Very well. I shall devise something. There are
sacks on the raft. We shall tranship. Meanwhile we can
return.

ALAN (*indicating* ASSISTANT) What about him?

ARTHUR He is in no state to be moved.

ALAN Do we come back for him?

ARTHUR Unless you would prefer to remain.

ALAN Shall I leave the water bottle?

ARTHUR If you wish.

LECTURER It was not the true voice I heard. When we were very thirsty, we drank the blood of the Shetland pony. I knew then it was not the true voice.

ALAN (*to* ASSISTANT) We'll be back. Just wait.

LECTURER Enough. Places.

> (ALAN *and* ARTHUR *begin to return to their chairs.*
> LECTURER *stops* ARTHUR, *who halts and half-turns*)
> Arthur!

ARTHUR Yes?

LECTURER What will you do with the old man?

ARTHUR Oh . . . Kill him, of course.

> (ARTHUR *proceeds to his chair*)

LECTURER (*to* AUDIENCE) They transhipped the grain. It took two days. On the second night, the ark caught fire.

> (LECTURER *nods to* ASSISTANT, *who gives a long scream.*
> *The cast have been sitting as if asleep on their chairs, but at the first scream* ALAN *wakes, listens, then moves forwards into the Main Cabin, and then on Deck. When he reaches the deck, he runs forward to the edge.* MURIEL *wakes, sees* ALAN *going, and follows him unobserved*)

ALAN The bastard! The rotten bastard!

MURIEL You shouldn't speak against Arthur like that.

ALAN Speak against him! Don't you see what he's done? Look at the ark burning. That's not an accident.

MURIEL Arthur does what he has to do.

ALAN And the old man?

MURIEL That's as may be.

ALAN Arthur's murdered him.

MURIEL Oh, yes. My husband too.

> (*Pause*)

ALAN What?

MURIEL Wesley too. You know that.

ALAN But Wesley . . . blew away.

50

MURIEL No. Arthur took care of that. I know. Arthur takes
what he wants. After all, he has to, hasn't he, if we're
to respect him?
(*She nods wisely, and goes back in.* ALAN *follows her.*
LECTURER *stops him*)
LECTURER Wait (ALAN *obeys*) Will you protest?
ALAN No.
LECTURER Tell me what you are thinking.
ALAN What's the point?
LECTURER Of what?
ALAN Human life. Everything. Look. (*Turning to him*)
You're born; you grow old; you die. You feed and sleep,
and go to work every week, and take a holiday once a
year. You raise children, and they grow up and leave
you, and you're left alone. Much of your life is spent
in discomfort, and more in boredom, and most in
indifference. All you have to expect is monotony and
struggle while you're working, and loneliness and fear
in your old age. And what's it all for? You don't really
believe that making things, and packing them up, and
moving them about, and selling them, and buying
them, and consuming them, and making new things to
replace them, add up to a reason for living. But you go
on—keeping alive, because you're afraid of death. If
Arthur knows what he wants, and why he wants it,
what can I do?
LECTURER You do not speak of your jealousy?
ALAN No. I watch. I listen. I try to overhear. (*Pause*) I
imagine.
LECTURER Why not speak to her?
ALAN We're never alone together.
LECTURER Miss Banks! (*To* ALAN) Now you are alone.
(SONYA *comes to* ALAN, *while*)
ALAN (*to* LECTURER) I remember . . . it's very faint what I
remember. Not clear. I know there was a time . . . I
know we weren't together for so long.
LECTURER Three weeks.
ALAN There's a lot before that I don't know . . . I don't

remember.

SONYA Three weeks.

ALAN (*to her*) Just drifting. Going hungry mostly. I remember that we were happy. We sang a lot. We made love.

SONYA Yes.

ALAN That first night.

SONYA I remember.

ALAN I'd never known anything like it. Sex had been—been *having* people—imposing myself. And pretending what I didn't really feel. I'd never felt so close. We're not close here. We're never even alone together.

SONYA We're alone now.

ALAN Someone might come.

(*Pause*)

SONYA What do you want to say?

(*Pause*)

Do you think I don't miss *you*? Do you think I don't want to be alone with *you*?

(*He comes to her tentatively. They kiss, at first tentatively, then more fiercely, then as closely as can be*)

ALAN (*a sort of laugh*) And they say a starvation diet keeps your thoughts off sex!

(*He begins gently to persuade her to the ground, but she pulls away*)

SONYA No. Not now.

ALAN Not?

SONYA Let's just . . . be together for a bit. Sex—it's not that important.

ALAN Oh, it is.

SONYA It's just sex. We can have sex any time.

ALAN No, we can't. You know bloody well we can't.

SONYA No, but . . . I mean, I don't see why it has to be the first thing . . . I mean, if two people love each other——

ALAN They make love.

SONYA They don't have to, that's the point. If they love each other, they don't *have* to.

ALAN But, love, I want to. We both want to. I ache for it.

52

SONYA I thought it'd be nice just to be together for a bit . . . sort of—comfy.

ALAN After.

SONYA We never talk. Not you and me. We never get the chance. Tony's the only person I ever talk to.

ALAN Ah, yes; Tony. You are alone with him, of course. Very convenient.

(*Pause*)

SONYA We don't have to be.

ALAN You don't encourage visitors.

SONYA What do you mean?

ALAN *I* didn't get much of a welcome. I was humiliated, as I remember.

SONYA Not humiliated.

ALAN What would you call it?

SONYA He was trying to help. (*Pause*) Anyway, why should we spend our time talking about Tony?

ALAN He interests me. (*Pause*) What *about* Tony anyway? How about him? Is sex the first thing in *his* mind, would you say?

SONYA Of course not.

ALAN Why not? He's not queer?

SONYA No.

ALAN Ah, you know that, then?

SONYA Sex doesn't come into it. I don't love Tony. We get on; that's all. He's more my kind of person than——

ALAN I am?

(*Pause*)

SONYA Yes, in a way. But I don't love him.

ALAN I don't see why that should stop you. If sex isn't that important.

SONYA I didn't mean that.

ALAN As far as I can see, your way of showing love for someone is *not* to have sex with him. So since you say you don't love Tony——

SONYA Stop it.

ALAN Yes, you're alone with Tony, aren't you? And do you think I don't wonder what you do together? Do you

53

think I don't sit here and wonder?

SONYA You know what we do. We do our exercises.

ALAN That's one way of describing it.

SONYA You stupid sod!

(*Pause*)

ALAN You could do your exercises up here. On deck.

SONYA We could, but we don't.

ALAN (*bursts out*) 'We!' 'We!' You and Tony aren't 'we'. You and I are 'we'.

SONYA Well, behave like it, then. Trust me for a start.

ALAN Trust!

SONYA Why should that be difficult?

ALAN I'll tell you.

SONYA Pray do.

ALAN You and I—we'd never met before I found you floating on that piano in Gloucestershire. We made love that same night. You didn't 'hold back' or anything. You didn't want just to 'be' together. Nothing like that. We dived into sex. We pulled it up over our heads, and drowned in it. And you were a bloody sight better than I was. More experienced. But I suppose that's because it was 'just sex', eh? Not *that* important.

SONYA And?

ALAN If me, why not Tony? If so *soon* with me, so quick with me?

(*Pause*)

SONYA I think I'll go in now. I've gone off you. Funny!—I came out to tell you something. It's rather important actually. I've been saving it to tell you. Nobody else knows.

ALAN Not even Tony?

SONYA I'm pregnant.

(*Pause*)

ALAN What?

SONYA I thought you'd be pleased. I was *that* stupid.

ALAN But I am. I am, love. I am. I am pleased

SONYA Are you? Well, that won't last, will it? After all, you don't know whose it is.

54

(She turns her back on him, and goes inside. He watches her)

LECTURER The water ration was reduced. Raw fish gave everyone diarrhoea. They grew weaker. The sun brought out self-doubts like bubbles on a tarred roof, which grew, and burst, and grew again. *(To* CAST*)* Days in the Sun. The Middle Time.

*(*HUNTER, GERTRUDE *and* BANNER *have appeared with chairs which they arrange for sunbathing.* ALAN *stays where he is.* TONY *and* SONYA *go into the hold area for their exercises.* MURIEL *watches* ALAN *and the sunbathers from a little distance)*

BANNER I found I couldn't communicate, do you see? There were problems of language. Among the criminal classes, the word 'bird' for instance, is used to mean 'lady friend' and also a stretch in prison. So that the expression 'to do one's bird' was only confusing.

GERTRUDE I played Antigone in the West End when I was only twenty-four. Gilbert Murray sent me orchids and Doctor Ernest Jones took me out to lunch.

*(*SONYA *laughs)*

MURIEL They're down there.

ALAN I know.

MURIEL They're always down there.

GERTRUDE Six years ago, I went back to the same theatre. My agent said it would be a come-back for me. I was the Vicar's wife in a comedy about sailors—not a large part, by no means large. I'd written 'Gertrude Forbes-Cooper, Actress' in greasepaint on the wall of my dressing-room. It was still there, so I crossed out the 'Actress'.

HUNTER I used to wonder what was going to happen to all the chaps like me. I mean, if you're not bright, where are you going to go? I used to look at middle-aged chaps in the tube, on buses; I used to think, '*You're* like me. *You're* not bright. You'll go under. Bound to.'

GERTRUDE The theatre! That feeling one had sometimes in the theatre, that wonderful thrill, almost of reverence, a

55

     pricking of the back hairs. . . .

BANNER Yes?

GERTRUDE I discovered it could be self-induced.

 BANNER But surely one learns from the theatre, does one not?

  ALAN Learns what?

 BANNER About the nature of life?

  ALAN You'd learn more about life from one week as a
    probation officer than ten years of heavy theatre-going.

 MURIEL We are in a bad temper, aren't we?

GERTRUDE Arthur sees these things so differently. It is a matter
    of proportion he says.

 BANNER Of control.

GERTRUDE Of seeing things in proportion.

 BANNER Control. Things had got out of hand. That is why I
    was able to do no good. Even the youth work—the
    only way one could avoid damages to the premises
    was to exclude undesirables, and these were the ones
    who most needed help. I became confused in my
    mind.

 HUNTER '*Down* you go,' I'd think. 'They'll automate the lot of
    you. Rabbits!'

 BANNER At last I began to doubt my own motives. I had to live
    from moment to moment, and hope I was right. But
    the doubts would always be waiting for me. Arthur
    says——

  ALAN Oh, Arthur! Arthur!

 BANNER It is a matter of control.

  ALAN How can Arthur or anyone else——

GERTRUDE Arthur will look after things. It is only a matter of
    obeying.

 MURIEL Arthur knows what's right.

 BANNER Exactly. Exactly.

  ALAN How? How does he know?

 HUNTER Well, I mean there's a place for everybody with Arthur.

 MURIEL Arthur knows what's best for all of us.

  ALAN A murderer!

    (*Silence.* ARTHUR *gets up from his chair*)

    Arthur's our leader, and we depend on him, but he's

not a god. He's not above doing foolish and wicked
things; you know that. It wouldn't have hurt us to
have taken that old man from the ark, but Arthur
murdered him.

(*Pause*)

BANNER How hot it is!

HUNTER Discipline must be maintained, you know.

GERTRUDE I remember that as a very *little* girl, I could lie all day
in the sun. Mother always said I was storing up energy
for the winter.

ALAN (*near tears*) You don't want to hear. You just lie here,
airing your bloody doubts, but you won't listen.
You're afraid of being upset.

GERTRUDE But we're not afraid of anything, while Arthur is here
to look after us.

(MURIEL *leaves the deck area, and goes to cabin. She
knocks*)

ARTHUR Come in, Mrs. Otterdale. (*She does so*) Make your
report.

MURIEL They're carrying on?

ARTHUR Who?

MURIEL That Sonya and Tony. *He* knows. He can't keep his
mind off it when they're down there.

ARTHUR No self-discipline. He deserves what he gets.

MURIEL What are you going to do about it, Arthur?

ARTHUR Permit it.

MURIEL But they're carrying on.

ARTHUR It is of no consequence. If Miss Banks is carrying on
now, she can have less objection to being shared later.

MURIEL Shall I be shared, Arthur?

ARTHUR Of course.

MURIEL (*a horrid little giggle*) It'll make a change. Will Gertrude
be——

ARTHUR All the women will be shared. In the New Society we
shall all love one another. Equally.

MURIEL But you most, Arthur.

ARTHUR First, Mrs. Otterdale, not most. There is a distinction.
What else do you have to tell me?

57

MURIEL He's been talking against you.

ARTHUR Mr. Armitage? In what way?

MURIEL He said you were a murderer. He said you did foolish and wicked things. He said you weren't a god.

ARTHUR Foolish?

MURIEL That's what he said.

ARTHUR What can he have meant by foolish?

MURIEL Foolish and wicked, he said. He told Harold and Gertrude.

ARTHUR What did they reply?

MURIEL They said it was very hot.

ARTHUR Foolish? I should be angry if I did not consider the source.

MURIEL What'll you do to him, then?

ARTHUR Nothing. He does no harm. Mr. Armitage is without a backbone and without convictions. When it comes to the point he will always do as he is told. Meanwhile we can use a cook. And you might look more closely at Miss Banks, my dear. She is concealing something.

MURIEL Yes, Arthur. (*Pause*) There's nothing else, Arthur.

ARTHUR Nothing?

MURIEL Unless . . . *you* wanted anything. . . .
(ARTHUR *takes her by the shoulders*)

ARTHUR You must not be coy, my dear. It is not becoming in a widow of your years.
(*He embraces her, in the manner of one who takes, but does not share*)

ARTHUR But you must be very quiet.
(*He kisses her again, then breaks away*)

ARTHUR Not a god, he said?

MURIEL I'll lie down, shall I?

LECTURER Enough. The evening meal now. (*As they take their places in the Saloon area; to* AUDIENCE) The change from an autocratic to a theocratic society began that evening at supper.

ARTHUR I have been thinking about myth.

GERTRUDE Myth. . . . Yes. . . .

ARTHUR We are all of us in a mythological situation, are we not?

BANNER Er . . .

ARTHUR We are the people who came out of the sea. A new race will spring, as it were, from our loins.

TONY Loins?

ALAN Sex.

ARTHUR Consider our descendants. For their own self-respect, they must remember us as greater than we are. *We* may know that we are quite ordinary beings——

GERTRUDE No, no, Arthur.

MURIEL Not you, Arthur.

HUNTER Not Arthur, by George.

ARTHUR Thank you. (*A little smile*) However.

BANNER Do please continue, Arthur.

ARTHUR We may know that we are human. But if we are to found a race, they may wish to think of us as gods. And it may be good for them to think so. It will encourage morality and right behaviour.

TONY Gods? Us?

ARTHUR And goddesses, of course. (*Permissive nod to the women*)

SONYA Thank you.

ARTHUR Cooks in the future may light a candle to Mr. Armitage. And as for me . . .

GERTRUDE Yes, Arthur.

ARTHUR Our descendants may think of *me* as the leader of all. The source of all power and benefits. They may do that.

GERTRUDE Oh, they will. They will.

ARTHUR What makes a god? Any thinking person will tell you that men make their own. They do so by worship. Whatever you worship is god, whether it be a tree, or the sun, or two sticks, or a bull, or a ring of stones. Simple men worship the things themselves. Complicated men worship the ideas the things express. But in terms of ultimate behaviour, it makes little difference. The behaviour—the ritual—is what matters. Interpretations may change, but the ritual endures. Is that not so, Mr. Banner?

BANNER Very largely, Arthur.

59

ARTHUR Very largely.

BANNER Entirely.

ARTHUR Good. (*Looks round the table*) You had better begin by worshipping me. Some of you may feel that I am unworthy. You must conquer that feeling. It will, in any case, die with you, while what is recorded of your behaviour will live on as revealed religion. Any questions?

(*Pause*)

ALAN No questions.

ARTHUR Then we shall begin our meal. Mr. Banner, please ask a blessing.

(BANNER *looks timidly at* ARTHUR, *who gives him an encouraging nod*)

BANNER For what we are about to receive, may Arthur make us truly thankful.

ARTHUR Quite right. And so I do.

(*Holds his arms out in benison*)

LECTURER They required a wind, so that the raft would be propelled through the sea, and its batteries be recharged, and they would have heat again to distil water, and cook their food. Arthur told them that they must behave in a manner appropriate to the myth in which they were participating. They must attempt to raise a wind by magic. They did so.

(GERTRUDE *goes to the upstage deck area where she beats at the foot of the imaginary mast, continuing to do this through the action until indicated. Meanwhile*)

They beat a wet rag against metal, but there was no wind.

(MURIEL *goes out on deck with an imaginary bowl of water and swooshes it round throughout the action, while*)

They filled a bowl with sea-water and rocked it about to make waves in sympathetic magic, but the waves lacked sympathy, and there was no wind.

(HUNTER *goes to the front of the deck area, and begins to whistle mournfully*)

They whistled.

(ALAN, TONY, BANNER *and* ARTHUR *join* HUNTER *in whistling*)

The men all whistled for a wind.

(SONYA *joins them and* GERTRUDE *and* MURIEL *begin to whistle where they are*)

And the women whistled for a wind, but the wind did not reply.

(ARTHUR *watches for a moment then*)

ARTHUR Stop. What next?

ALAN They used to nail a gold piece to the mast.

ARTHUR They?

ALAN People. Primitive people.

ARTHUR Mr. Batch, pray instruct Miss Forbes-Cooper to cease whistling and join us. Perhaps someone has a gold piece with them?

(*Pause. Nobody has*)

Or any gold object?

MURIEL I've got two pounds.

ARTHUR Yes.

MURIEL Nine and seven.

ARTHUR Get it. Captain Hunter, pray fetch a hammer, proceed to the mast and prepare to nail.

(HUNTER *goes off to the hold area for a hammer and a nail.* MURIEL *feels furtively inside her clothing and gets out imaginary money, while*)

ALAN They threw money into the sea too. A sort of offering.

ARTHUR (*taking money from* MURIEL) Then we shall divide the money. Mr. Batch, you will assist Captain Hunter to nail this pound note as high up the mast as possible. Mount his shoulders. We shall throw the remaining one pound nine and seven simultaneously into the sea. Is there anything else, Mr. Armitage, while you think of it?

ALAN Not unless you have anybody in mind for Iphigenia.

ARTHUR Iphigenia? I don't understand you.

ALAN Oh, it wasn't a serious suggestion. I'm afraid you'd need a real child if you were going to sacrifice to——

(*He stops himself, horrified.* SONYA's *hands have gone to*

61

her belly. They gaze at each other. ARTHUR *notices.*
BANNER does not and chunters on)

BANNER The reference, Arthur, is to King Agamemnon, who
  sacrificed his own daughter when the Greeks lay
  becalmed at Aulis.

ALAN I said it wasn't a serious suggestion.
  (HUNTER *to the mast with an imaginary hammer and*
  nail. TONY *gets up on his shoulders and prepares to nail*
  the pound note while ARTHUR *draws the rest of the crew*
  into a half-circle to watch him offer the money)

ARTHUR Ready, Mr. Batch?

TONY O.K.

ARTHUR Right. I suppose notes will be acceptable.
  (*He throws the money.* TONY *hammers. The rest watch)*

GERTRUDE How pretty the half-crowns look, turning over and
  over—oh!

SONYA What?

GERTRUDE A fish has eaten the pound note.

ARTHUR A fish has eaten the pound note. The gift has been
  accepted. But I imagine that we must wait a while.
  (TONY *and* HUNTER *return)*

TONY Hey, Arthur!

ARTHUR Yes?

TONY I saw something. Looked like fog or something.

ARTHUR Fog? Impossible.

TONY Or smoke or something. A sort of wall, all thick and
  cloudy. It's over there. Look.

ALAN (*sarcastic dislike for* TONY) A forest fire, perhaps?

TONY What's so funny? It could be something burning. I
  mean, *we* burned——
  (*Hiss of indrawn breath from* BANNER, GERTRUDE *and*
  MURIEL)

ARTHUR What? What did 'we' burn?

TONY I'm not trying to make nothing of it.

ARTHUR Then avoid the impression that you are. (*He gets up*
  on to one of the chairs for a better view) It does appear
  to be fog. And moving, as I suppose, towards us, since
  we do not move.

SONYA Yes. You can see it now. From down here.
>   (*They move towards the edge of the raft, as if the fog were approaching them from the audience*)

HUNTER Never seen fog like that before. Nothing like it in the *Children's Encyclopaedia*.

BANNER Out of . . . a clear sky.

HUNTER I dare say there's an explanation if we looked it up.

BANNER Drift . . . sea-drift. . . .

HUNTER You'd look in the index. Under F I dare say.

BANNER The edge of the world was held by the ancients to be a place of fogs.
>   (GERTRUDE *and* MURIEL *are frightened. They move closer to* ARTHUR)

ARTHUR The world is round. It has no edge.

BANNER No . . . no, of course not.

GERTRUDE It is a little like 'Outward Bound'. When one makes the crossing between this world and the next.

SONYA I saw a picture about Niagara Falls once. They were all steamy. Marilyn Monroe was in it.

ALAN It's much closer now.

HUNTER Be in it soon, eh?

MURIEL Arthur!

GERTRUDE Arthur, make her be quiet.

MURIEL I wish we'd never come. I wish we'd stayed at home. We don't know how thick it is or anything.

LECTURER (*to* FIRST ASSISTANT) Noise, please.
>   (ASSISTANT *goes offstage, while*)

ALAN (*angry*) There's nothing to be frightened of. We've all flown through cloud before.

TONY What's a cloud doing down here, then?
>   (*A noise begins. It is a high noise on one note. It gets louder as the scene progresses, cutting out when indicated. As it begins, they listen*)

LECTURER (*to* CAST) With the noise, the water becomes suddenly choppy.
>   (*All stagger*)

ARTHUR This is ridiculous. There is no wind to inspire rough water.

63

HUNTER Hey! The water's changing colour.

(*They shift the focus of their attention downwards*)

SONYA It's all brown.

GERTRUDE (*a wail*) The water's poisoned. Arthur!

MURIEL It's the drowned people, poisoning the water.

ARTHUR Nonsense. It is only weed. A common phenomenon at sea. Brown weed.

ALAN We've never seen weed before. Not like this. Covering the sea.

ARTHUR You see it now.

(*Pause*)

SONYA I wish I knew what the noise was.

LECTURER (*to* CAST) A moment. (*They are still; to* AUDIENCE) They had, of course, come to what is indeed a common enough phenomenon at sea—the meeting of two currents, one warm, one cold. All this time they had thought themselves motionless, they had been drifting with one current. Now they had come to the junction, and found mist there, and a great deal of weed, and a high concentration of marine life, most of it in violent activity. (*To* CAST) Continue.

ARTHUR I have worked things out. We are in a current. We have been drifting, and without a point of reference, could not know it.

BANNER (*sneezes*)

ALAN Bless you.

BANNER Thank you.

ARTHUR Surely we were more warmly clad when we came aboard?

MURIEL Will I get your oilskins, Arthur?

ARTHUR No. Blankets. Blankets for all. Miss Forbes-Cooper, assist her.

(*They go to the indoors area, where* FIRST ASSISTANT *and* SECOND ASSISTANT *give them blankets*)

HUNTER Hallo!

ARTHUR What was that?

(HUNTER *goes to see, and as he does so, another lurch makes them all stagger. He picks up an imaginary fish*)

HUNTER It's a fish. Jumped right out of the water and on to the deck. Silly little bastard must have lost his way in the fog.

(GERTRUDE *and* MURIEL *reappear with blankets*)

ARTHUR One to each, please.

HUNTER What shall I do with the fish?

ALAN Eat it!

HUNTER Better to throw it back. It's undersized anyway.

(*All have been given blankets and wear them round their shoulders*)

ARTHUR Has everyone been issued with blankets?

SONYA We do look like a lot of Red Indians, I must say.

BANNER It's getting . . . thicker.

MURIEL Arthur, will it finish soon?

ARTHUR Stay close to me, Mrs. Otterdale, if you are frightened.

GERTRUDE I'm frightened too.

ARTHUR Very well. You may come close also.

SONYA That noise is louder too.

BANNER I don't understand the noise. I confess I do not.

(*Another lurch—though they have been a little unsteady ever since the choppiness of the water was remarked*)

ALAN I'm not used to this. I don't feel very well.

ARTHUR Stay close to the side, then, and do not soil the deck.

SONYA I'm so cold.

(ALAN *has an idea. He dips his hand over the side*)

ALAN The water's cold. It's been warm all this time.

GERTRUDE (*a wail*) I'm frightened.

MURIEL (*joining in*) Frightened!

(*They take* ARTHUR'*s hands. He tries to break their hold*)

ARTHUR Mrs. Otterdale! Miss Forbes-Cooper! Let go of my hands.

GERTRUDE We're frightened.

MURIEL Frightened.

ARTHUR I must retain my freedom of action. Go inside, ladies.

MURIEL (*sobs*) I can't. If I can't see, I don't know what I shan't imagine.

GERTRUDE Can't go in. Don't make us go in.

(LECTURER *now moves to them and speaks to them sharply and urgently*)

LECTURER Fish! Fish everywhere. Jumping and leaping. Hunting and hunted. Eating and being eaten. The air and the water, thick with fish and mist, all alive, all everywhere —screaming, screaming all around. That is what you hear. You hear the fish scream.

MURIEL I want to go home. I want to go home.

(GERTRUDE *claps her hands on her breast as though a fish has jumped at her. All the following dialogue overlaps*)

(GERTRUDE *screams*)

What is it? Oh, what is it?

GERTRUDE Arthur! Save me? Arthur!

(GERTRUDE *tries to clasp* ARTHUR, *who tries to avoid her.* MURIEL, *jealous as well as frightened, tries to pull her off, and clasp* ARTHUR *for herself.* HUNTER *and* BANNER *are trying to calm them down.* SONYA *moves away, her hands over her belly to protect it. Both* ALAN *and* TONY *come to her, but both stop, on meeting the other. Noise continues, louder. Overlapping dialogue. A mess*)

HUNTER It's only a fish. It's harmless.

MURIEL Leave Arthur alone. You leave him alone.

ARTHUR Miss Forbes-Cooper! Mrs. Otterdale!

GERTRUDE Save me! Save me! You promised.

MURIEL You keep off him. He's mine.

HUNTER Harold, tell her it's only a fish.

GERTRUDE Arthur!

ARTHUR Unhand me.

HUNTER (*tossing fish away*) It's harmless. It couldn't hurt you.

ARTHUR Mr. Banner! Captain Hunter! Get rid of these women.

BANNER Come on now, Gertrude.

GERTRUDE Won't go. Don't make me go.

HUNTER ⎫
BANNER ⎭ Come on. (*Pulling*)

GERTRUDE ⎫
MURIEL ⎭ No! No! (*Resisting*)

MURIEL (*to* ARTHUR) You're God! You told us. Make it stop.

GERTRUDE God. You're God.

66

MURIEL God! God! Make it stop.

GERTRUDE God make it stop.

> (*A pause while the men wait for* ARTHUR *to respond. All talk has to be loud above the noise, but* ALAN *now says savagely*)

ALAN Go on, Arthur. Make it stop, if you're God.

> (*Pause*)

ARTHUR Let go your hands, women. Take your hands from my robe.

> (*The women let go. All watch* ARTHUR. *He goes to the edge of the deck area, spreads his blanket like wings from his shoulders, and addresses the audience area*)
>
> Waters! By virtue of the authority vested in me as God, I command you to stop.
>
> (*A small pause. Then the noise cuts out*)
>
> I will have no more nonsense, waters. I command it.
>
> (*Pause*) Now, go forth, and feel the waters, Mr. Armitage.
>
> (ALAN *does so*)

ALAN They're warm again.

BANNER God be praised.

> (ARTHUR *turns and looks at him*)
>
> God Arthur be praised, that is.

ARTHUR We shall go in now. There is nothing more to do here.

> (*Wearing his blanket like a robe, he walks upstage. The others fall in behind him, making a procession. The procession goes offstage completely.* LECTURER *steps forward*)

LECTURER From that time, a small wind blew from the south-west. It was enough to move the raft, and recharge the batteries, so that they had water again, and warm food. From that time also, they had company always with them—a small company of sharks who followed the raft wherever it went.

> (LECTURER *leaves stage*)

END OF ACT TWO

ACT THREE

All the characters but ARTHUR *are on their chairs; he remains offstage.* ASSISTANTS *have removed un-needed and set needed props.* LECTURER *arrives. House lights down.*

LECTURER The miracle by which Arthur proved his godhead was not really a miracle. The raft had passed out of the junction area of the two currents: that is all. But to the people of the raft—and certainly to Arthur himself—it did seem miraculous. Meanwhile the sun shone. The days passed. Miss Banks's condition became obvious, and was accepted.

(*An* ASSISTANT *comes to* SONYA *and motions her to stand. He fastens to her stomach a kind of small bolster, tying it with tapes at the back. She runs her hand wonderingly over it, as if feeling the baby within her belly. While*) There were no more exercises, though she continued to spend time with Mr. Batch.

SONYA (*begins to sing 'Flow Gently Sweet Afton' like a lullaby to herself*)

TONY What's that, then?

SONYA 'Flow Gently Sweet Afton.' Don't you know it? Come out in the sun. I'll teach you.

(SONYA *and* TONY *find a place together on the deck area, while*)

LECTURER The god Arthur remained incommunicado. He was growing a beard, as became his godhead. As the only clergyman, Mr Banner became priest to the god. He prepared the god's food, and was the only one allowed to see the god.

(BANNER *rises and mimes a business in the kitchen area, while*)

Mr. Armitage continued to cook for the others.

(ALAN *goes to the entrance of the kitchen area and watches*

68

BANNER *disdainfully. While)*
Drifting gently in the warm water, remote from any
society but their own, with a god now to look after
them, each in his own way moved back into childhood:
it was so easy. (*Gently to* MURIEL) Play, Muriel. Go
out and play now.
(*Solemnly* MURIEL *goes out on deck, and begins to mime
playing a bouncing-ball game against the imaginary wall
of the cabin*)

MURIEL (*sings*) Bouncy, bouncy, ball-ie!
Break a leg of doll-ie.

LECTURER Gertrude!

MURIEL (*sings*) One an' two an' three an' four an' five an'
six (*etc.*).
(GERTRUDE *gets up during* MURIEL's *chant and begins to
rummage in a corner of the saloon area*)

GERTRUDE Harold.

BANNER Yes?

GERTRUDE Do you want a game?

BANNER Draughts or halma.

GERTRUDE Draughts, of course, silly billy.

BANNER No.

GERTRUDE Halma then.

BANNER I can't. I've got to get the god his lunch.

ALAN I'll play.

GERTRUDE No. I want to play with Harold.
(BANNER *has carried an imaginary plate in from the
kitchen area, and sets it on the table*)

ALAN Suit yourself.

BANNER (*to* GERTRUDE) Help me on with my surplice.
(ALAN *goes on outside.* BANNER *gets his surplice on,
helped by* GERTRUDE, *and carries the imaginary plate to
the cabin area. While*)

MURIEL I did thirty-one.

ALAN Good.

MURIEL You don't care, do you?

ALAN No.

MURIEL Bet you can't do thirty-one. Bet you can't do any.

69

ALAN (*looking round*) Where's Hunter?

MURIEL In the toilet. He's always there; it's not fair. You can't get in. He doesn't do anything. He just sits there, sucking his thumb.

(BANNER *mimes knocking*)

BANNER The servant of the god, with the god's lunch.

LECTURER Enter and wait. You see the god before you.

(BANNER *enters the upstairs area and waits*)

SONYA (*sings*) Flow gently, sweet Afton,
    Among thy green braes.

TONY What's braes, then?

SONYA I don't know. It's just in the song. (*Sings*)
    Flow gently,
    I'll sing thee a song in thy praise.

(MURIEL *has been watching and has come to stand over them. Now she begins to sing in competition*)

MURIEL (*sings*) Root them up. Put them behind,
    Four little foxes that will spoil the vine.

SONYA Shut up. I'm trying to teach Tony a song.

MURIEL Who's stopping you?

SONYA He can't concentrate on one song, if you're singing another.

MURIEL Sucks! Boo! Boodleie-hoo! I've got a better song than you.

TONY (*says*) Flow Gently. I'll sing thee a song in thy praise.

MURIEL (*sings*) Envy! Jealousy! Malice! Pride!
    All if allowed will in your heart abide.

(ALAN *shrugs and goes back into the saloon area*)

ALAN What's the god having for lunch?

GERTRUDE Well, Harold *calls* it bouillabaisse. What are we having?

ALAN Flying fish.

SONYA (*sings*) Flow gently, sweet Afton, among thy green braes.
    Flow gently, I'll sing thee a song in thy praise.

TONY (*says*) Song in thy praise.

MURIEL (*sings*) All if allowed will in your heart abide.

ALAN We get better food than the god does because I'm a better cook than Harold is.

GERTRUDE (*shocked*) Harold isn't a cook at all. He's the priest of

the god. You are awful, saying that. Harold doesn't
cook. He prepares the god's repast. *You* cook.
(LECTURER *signs to* ASSISTANT, *who goes into the cabin
area and whispers to* BANNER. *While*)

SONYA (*sings*) My Mary's asleep by thy murmuring stream.

TONY (*says*) —ring stream.

SONYA (*sings*) Flow gently, sweet Afton. Disturb not her dream.
(BANNER *comes out of the cabin area to the Saloon*)

BANNER The god wants some glue.

ALAN What's he want glue for?

BANNER He didn't say.

GERTRUDE It's better not to question the god's desires. Whatever
the god wants is good.

BANNER He may have a use for glue. On the other hand, he may
just want it.

ALAN There's some in the hold. I'll get it.

BANNER No. I'll go. Otherwise it would only have to be purified.

GERTRUDE Now we'll miss our game.

BANNER (*going*) The service of the god comes before games.
(BANNER *mimes the business of going down into the hold
and searching about. While*)

ALAN I said I'd play. Let me play. Why can't I play?

GERTRUDE We'll keep a separate score, then. One for you and one
for Harold. There's no point in playing unless you can
see who's won.
(*They carry their imaginary box of draughts out on to the
deck and set up the board, while*)

SONYA Now go all through by yourself.

TONY (*sings*) Flow gently, sweet Afton, among thy green . . .
(*Stops*)

SONYA (*prompts*) Braes.

TONY (*sings*) Flow gently, I'll . . . I'll sing thee . . .

SONYA (*prompts, singing*) A song in thy praise.

ALAN Can't you shut up singing that? It puts me off.

MURIEL (*with relish*) Envy! Jealousy! Malice! Pride!

TONY (*sings*) My Mary's asleep by thy murmuring stream.

MURIEL (*sings*) All if allowed will in your heart abide.

GERTRUDE You've got to take me. And now (*moving piece*) I . . .

71

take . . . you. You're not much good, are you?

ALAN I can't concentrate with Tony caterwauling all the time.
BANNER *has come out of the hold. He goes into the saloon area, and then to cabin, and knocks. While)*

BANNER The servant of the god with glue.
(He enters. Pause. ASSISTANT *whispers. While)*

GERTRUDE Shouldn't have asked to play, then.

ALAN Oh, for Christ's sake, why does everybody keep getting at me all the time?

GERTRUDE Who's getting at you? *I'm* not getting at you.

MURIEL She's not getting at you.

ALAN *(mimicking)* 'Shouldn't have asked to play, then.' It's no pleasure playing with you.

GERTRUDE Alan, don't struggle. You're not happy within yourself. (BANNER *receives the message, comes into the saloon, then out on deck. While)*

ALAN *(angry)* Yes, I am. I'm quite happy.

GERTRUDE If you were happy in yourself, you'd see that the god Arthur is good and necessary, as we do.

BANNER Just make an act of faith, dear boy. Everything follows from that.

GERTRUDE You'll be a different man.

ALAN I don't want to be a different man.

BANNER Don't you? Are you enjoying life as you are?

ALAN What's he want with glue?

BANNER We are to make a mask.

MURIEL Can I help? I can help, can't I? I'll help.

BANNER We can all help, as an act of devotion. We soak paper in glue, and it turns into papier mâché. Then we mould it.

ALAN What does he want a mask for?

MURIEL Questions! Always asking questions!

BANNER He says his face is too terrible for us to see.

ALAN What's happened to his face?

GERTRUDE It is the face of a god. Of course it's terrible. It must be.

ALAN Harold sees it.

BANNER Not lately. He covers it under the sheet. He says

72

we're to make eyeholes and a mouth. This is going to
be a smiling mask, but later on we may have to make
a frowning one.

GERTRUDE Oh, Harold, I hope he will never appear to us in a
frowning mask.

MURIEL Not to us, but he may to some.

LECTURER (*to* ASSISTANTS) Bring on the god.

(ASSISTANTS *go offstage. Characters face upstage in
silence, and wait,* LECTURER *continues*)
They soaked pages of the Shell Guide to Bedfordshire
in a pot with glue, and made a mask. The god kept to
his own small room, and was not seen outside.

(ASSISTANTS *bring* ARTHUR *on. He is masked and his
beard protrudes outside the mask. He walks like a
sleepwalker, guided by the* ASSISTANTS, *who stand him on
his stool. While*)
It was hot in the god's holy place, and close, and being
a god, he could not wash or visit the lavatory, except
privately, so the atmosphere became unpleasant.

(BANNER *marshals all the others except* HUNTER *in a
group outside the upstairs area. While*)
Mr Banner brought the worshippers into the god's
presence.

BANNER Now, remember. When you get into the presence,
kneel, and bow your heads.

(*He looks around for* HUNTER, *sees him still sitting on his
chair against the back wall, and goes to get him.* HUNTER
pulls imaginary chain. BANNER *pushes and pulls him into
position.* HUNTER *moves like a small child, and sucks his
thumb, when he is in position*)

BANNER Ready?

SONYA It's so hot inside.

BANNER Follow me.

SONYA I don't feel very well.

BANNER (*irritated*) Really! Some people!

SONYA (*to* ALAN) I feel funny.

(BANNER *mimes knocking, calls out, and opens the door*)

BANNER (*intones*) The worshippers approach, god Arthur. All

73

make reverence before thee.

(*They go in, much crowded together.* BANNER *motions them to kneel. They do so,* GERTRUDE *helping* HUNTER, *who gives the god a military salute. Great squash and discomfort. While*)

LECTURER There was some defect in the construction of the mask. It made the god sound as if he had no roof to his mouth. Mr. Banner, as priest of the god, supplied a running translation.

ARTHUR Hee ha hee ho high.

BANNER The god tells us we shall see great things.

GERTRUDE (*whispers to* HUNTER) Great things.

(MURIEL *shushes her*)

ARTHUR Hi ha hay hahee ho hoo.

BANNER He has a surprise for us.

SONYA (*whispers*) So *hot*!

BANNER Ssssh!

ALL Sssssh!

ALAN (*whispers*) I'll take her out.

BANNER (*whispers*) You will not.

ARTHUR Ha hee ha ha hi——

ALAN (*whispers*) She's not well.

BANNER The god says——

ARTHUR (*repeats*) Ha hee ha ha hi——

(SONYA *keels over in a faint. Silence. The others look at her, and then frightened at the god.* ARTHUR *looks down at her*)

ARTHUR Ha hee ha ho.

BANNER A miracle.

ARTHUR Hee ha hee ho ho. Hy hee heahess ho he ho.

BANNER She has been overcome by the nearness of the god.

ALAN What should I do about it!

ARTHUR Ha ee hou.

BANNER Take her out.

ARTHUR He hive he.

BANNER Revive her.

(ALAN *looks around helplessly, then picks* SONYA *up in his arms, and carries her out, while*)

74

MURIEL Saucy! Putting herself forward.

GERTRUDE Ssssh!

BANNER (*motions to bow her head again*) Not if the god willed it, Mrs. Otterdale. (*Looks at* ARTHUR *for confirmation*)

ARTHUR Ha hee.

BANNER He did.

ARTHUR Hee hus hraie.

BANNER Let us pray.

(*Silence from the upstairs area, as they pray.* ALAN *sets* SONYA *in the deck area. She holds him*)

ALAN Are you O.K. eh, love? Are you?

SONYA What's going to become of me?

ALAN You'll be all right.

SONYA The time's so near.

ALAN I promise.

SONYA No doctor or nothing. Alan, I'm frightened.

ALAN We'll all help. I read a book. Natural Birth—it's often done. Love, we'll all——

SONYA Bloody *Children's Encyclopaedia*.

ALAN No, love. There's the women; they——

SONYA Not Muriel.

(*Pause*)

ALAN No. Not Muriel. I'll keep her away.

(*From the cabin area,* MURIEL *gives a scream, falls down, froths and rolls about.* ALAN *and* SONYA *hear this and look, scared and puzzled, in that direction. Overlapping dialogue—*ARTHUR *gives roofless commands, which* BANNER *translates as* 'Remove her. . . . Loosen her clothing. . . . She has been possessed . . .' *While* GERTRUDE *pushes* HUNTER *towards a chair, and out of the way. —All this very quick and more noise than dialogue.* BANNER *and* TONY *carry* MURIEL *into the saloon area, and lay her out on the table.* GERTRUDE *joins them*)

BANNER (*to* GERTRUDE) She has been possessed. You often hear of such cases in the United States.

(*Pause. Broken by* LECTURER)

LECTURER (*to* AUDIENCE) I have used the words 'the god' so far because it seems that this is what Arthur sincerely

75

believed himself to be. But it was, as I've said, hot in the holy place, and the air was offensive, and the circumstances uncomfortable. A god would not have minded such matters.

(*He has walked easily to the cabin area and stands behind* ARTHUR. *While*)

But Arthur minded. There was a small persistent voice inside that spoke to him. It was the voice of his own doubt. As he grew more uncomfortable, the voice became more insistent and more persuasive. I speak now as the voice of Arthur's doubt. (*To* ARTHUR) Can it be that you have made an elementary theological error?

ARTHUR Hee hoh.

LECTURER Yes, it is hot. And horrid in every way. A god could not be uncomfortable. But you are. Can it be that you are not the god?

ARTHUR (*reacts away*) Hi ha. Hi ha.

LECTURER Consider if the god were only to inhabit you, then he could, at any time, leave. (*Pause*) No man could carry the god within him for ever. The god would not wish it. (*Pause*) Only for a time. To those found worthy.

(*To* CAST) Supper. October 10th.

(*Place for supper*)

BANNER (*has an imaginary plate*) I'll just take the god his first fruits, and be back directly.

(BANNER *bears the plate to the cabin area, mimes knocking, enters with the imaginary plate which he makes a ceremony of laying at the god's feet. While*)

MURIEL The god doesn't care for flying fish.

GERTRUDE How do *you* know?

MURIEL The god likes us to take trouble. We don't catch flying fish; they catch themselves. They fly on board during the night, and all we do is pick them up in the morning. You can't call that first fruits when there's no trouble in it.

GERTRUDE You're not an authority on what the god likes.

MURIEL Yes, I am.

76

GERTRUDE Just because you say you've been possessed——
   MURIEL I have been possessed.
GERTRUDE —that doesn't make you an authority.
        (BANNER *has returned*)
   BANNER Well, the god has been pleased to accept our little
        offering, and now we can all tuck in.
GERTRUDE See? He does like flying fish.
   MURIEL He respects our feelings.
GERTRUDE The god doesn't have to respect our feelings. We're
        supposed to respect him and his feelings. If he didn't
        like flying fish, he'd throw them back. Isn't that right,
        Harold?
   BANNER Well——
   MURIEL I don't pay any mind to you. You're jealous.
GERTRUDE What have I got to be jealous about?
   MURIEL Because the god possessed me.
GERTRUDE I was possessed a long time before you were, if you
        want to know. The god possessed me before he *was* a
        god.
    ALAN Gertrude, you never told us.
   MURIEL He was always a god. We didn't know it before.
GERTRUDE Well, then?
   MURIEL Well then, what?
GERTRUDE He was a god when he possessed me, then.
   MURIEL He never possessed you.
GERTRUDE I know whether I was possessed or not.
   BANNER Ladies! Ladies!
   MURIEL Shut up!
   BANNER Mrs. Otterdale!
   MURIEL Be quiet. You're only the priest, but *I* was possessed.
GERTRUDE Why do you let her walk all over you, Harold?
   MURIEL I don't pay any mind to you. Jealous bitch!
GERTRUDE Bitch! Did you call me a bitch?
        (GERTRUDE *rises. She picks up an imaginary plate*)
LECTURER (*to* ARTHUR) The god stirs within you. You feel him
        uncoil within you.
   MURIEL Bitch.
   BANNER No. Don't throw anything. I'll tell the god.

GERTRUDE (*is shaking*) I've some pride left, Harold. I won't be
insulted in front of everyone. I've had a lot of cruelty
and inconsiderateness to put up with in my life, because
I've always said what I thought and not pretended.
I've sat alone in a tiny room——

MURIEL Bitch! Bitch!

GERTRUDE —waiting for the phone to ring. I've eaten dirt. I've
been refused. I've watched my own pupils pretend not
to see me in the foyers of theatres. I've been ignored in
the street.

BANNER Now, Gertrude!

GERTRUDE What right has that woman to insult me?—tell me that.
She falls down in a fit and calls it possession.

MURIEL That'll do from you. You keep your place. If the god
prefers me to you, then you ought to take your
medicine, and keep quiet about it, instead of——

GERTRUDE Oh! You!
(*She throws her imaginary plate.* MURIEL *dodges*)

LECTURER (*to* ARTHUR) He will go now. He will leave you now.
(GERTRUDE *and* MURIEL *square up to each other,
preparing to fight*)

BANNER Ladies!

ALAN Give over, Gertrude.

TONY I seen some lady wrestlers once. They had mud all
over them.
(MURIEL *launches an attack.*
BANNER *flaps about, without actually touching them.*
HUNTER *points his finger childishly at the two women and
begins to laugh*)

LECTURER (*to* ARTHUR) Now!

ARTHUR (*a long scream*)
(*All activity in the saloon area stops dead. All look,
shocked, towards the upstairs area*)

LECTURER (*to* ARTHUR) He is going . . . going . . . He goes back.

ARTHUR (*a continuous whimpering*)

LECTURER He has gone.
(ARTHUR *is still.* LECTURER *signs to* ASSISTANTS, *who
come to him, remove his mask. While*)

78

ALAN You'd better go and see what's happened.

BANNER I don't want to. I'm frightened.

(ARTHUR *walks briskly into the saloon area. Silence. He looks about him, at the women, and the imaginary plate*)

ARTHUR Why are there broken plates upon the floor?

(*Pause. All look at each other*)

BANNER (*timidly*) Thy servants fought amongst themselves.

GERTRUDE (*a little bob*) I'm sorry, god Arthur. The woman provoked me and I did throw a plate at her.

ARTHUR I am not the god, Arthur. The god Arthur has gone back to heaven. I am his vicar here on earth. (*To* BANNER) So you may remove that surplice. Mr. Banner. I shall be the god's high priest from now on. (*Pause*)

LECTURER (*to* CAST) Evening Service.

(*All but* ARTHUR *bring chairs out to the deck area* (HUNTER *as always being guided and helped*), *and sit in a row.* ARTHUR *watches, waits until they are ready, then takes the ship's log from the table and comes out to them standing before them as the priest. While*)

(*To* AUDIENCE) They had a service every evening, out on the deck. It began with a reading from what had once been the ship's log, then became the Minutes of the New Society, and was now the Book of Arthur. After the reading the high priest would expound.

ARTHUR (*reads*) There came a great wind over the surface of the waters, and the waters rose up, and the face of the sky was made black by the waters, and the voice of the god Arthur was heard in the wind, crying, 'Woe! Woe! to the sons of men.' Then many of those who were not of the Selected were swallowed up. They and their wives, their children and their beasts, both of the greater and the lesser sort, were swallowed up.

(ASSISTANT *makes a plopping noise with his mouth. Heads turn*)

But over the Selected, the god held the shield of his hand, and all save one—being judged unworthy—were saved by the god.

79

TONY (*quiet: to* SONYA) What one?

SONYA (*whispers*) Wesley.

TONY Oh!

    (ASSISTANT—*a whole series of plops. Heads turn*)

BANNER High Priest, Arthur?

ARTHUR Yes?

BANNER May I be permitted to draw your attention to a natural phenomenon, doubtless sent to us by the god. . . .

    (ARTHUR *walks to the edge of the deck area, looking down into the front rows of stalls*)

ARTHUR Extraordinary! (*To the others*) The reading is over.

BANNER (*timidly*) May we remain and observe the phenomenon?

ARTHUR Very well. We shall remain and await a sign.

LECTURER The night of the squid is confused in Armitage's account. At first there were only little squid, packed together in large numbers, covering the surface of the sea. Our forefathers stayed on deck, watching. It became dark. (*To* CAST) Dark. (*To* AUDIENCE) A little thread of wind came up to chill them.

SONYA Cold.

LECTURER Captain Hunter, what do you see?

HUNTER Lots of jolly little brown cobblestones. All over. You could walk to land if you knew where it was.

LECTURER No, after that.

HUNTER (*a scream*)

LECTURER Muriel? Harold? Gertrude?

MURIEL Squiggly. Squiggly things.

BANNER Black.

GERTRUDE Snakes. Horrid black snakes.

LECTURER Touching. Exploring. Pulling.

    (*It is as if the raft had tilted.* CAST *all lean one way*)

MURIEL Nasty pulls us.

BANNER Demon.

ALAN Don't sit there. Hit them. Get them away.

ARTHUR He has laid his hand on the raft and we feel the weight of it.

ALAN He?

LECTURER He! You see him. A squid. A giant squid. . . . Two

80

great tentacles and eight smaller ones, clustered about a giant head.

BANNER Sea-demon.

GERTRUDE Horrid. Nasty snakes. Beaky things.

LECTURER Pulling. Nearer and nearer.

ALAN We could get indoors. Why don't we get indoors.

BANNER High Priest Arthur, pray exorcise the demon before it eats us.

ARTHUR My fate cries out. (*He moves towards* LECTURER)

LECTURER Stop. It lets you go. (*Tilt reversed. To* AUDIENCE) The creature had tired of playing with the raft, and now disappeared.

(*All but* ARTHUR *dance like children*)

GERTRUDE (*cries out*) It's let us go.

ALAN Pushed us away.

SONYA It's gone. It's really gone.

HUNTER (*suddenly roars with laughter*) Pushed us away! Old sea-thing didn't want us, and pushed us away.

(ARTHUR *has been remaining still, apart from the others. Now he turns*)

ARTHUR Be quiet.

(*Pause*)

MURIEL Arthur? You'll talk to the god? You won't let that sea-thing come back?

BANNER Of course he won't.

GERTRUDE We must trust Arthur. He is all we have.

BANNER And very powerful with the god.

MURIEL You'll talk to him? I don't like that sea-thing.

(*Pause*)

ARTHUR Woman, that *was* the god. And he will come again.

(*Pause*)

BANNER The god?

ARTHUR Yes. I had no power over him. You saw that.

BANNER But what does he want?

ARTHUR I cannot say. But he will come again.

ALAN It was only a squid. You know that bloody well. Frightening the women! It was a giant squid—that's all.

ARTHUR The god can take many forms. He can take the form of a man or a squid. But in any form, he is terrible.

ALAN Oh, for Christ's sake, you don't really believe in all that!

(ARTHUR *steps forward and hits him. Then he turns and goes inside to the cabin area, followed by* BANNER. *All the others but* SONYA *and* TONY *follow him inside, but sit on their chairs on the back wall.* SONYA *hesitates, as if to stay with* ALAN)

ALAN No. You go in. I'm in disgrace.

(SONYA *goes*)

ALAN Bloody madness!

TONY Oh, I dunno.

ALAN You're not going in?

TONY Thought I might stay out here for a bit. I like watching the water. Relaxes you.

ARTHUR There is no place for blasphemers.

TONY (*indicating stalls*) Funny!—they've gone now. All them little squid. Well, they've not gone, I suppose! We've gone. Moved on past them. I often come out here and watch. Sonn and me, we——

ALAN Why don't you leave me alone?

ARTHUR Get him.

(BANNER *leaves* ARTHUR)

TONY Sharks is still there, mind. They're always there. Patient. Tagging along. You'd think they'd get tired.

(BANNER *comes on to the deck area*)

BANNER The High Priest wants to see you in the temple. He's very angry. He says there's no place for blasphemers among the Selected. I'd make an act of contrition if I were you.

ALAN You think he'll have me thrown to the sharks?

BANNER I hope not.

(*Silence.* ALAN *stares at* BANNER)

ALAN But that was a joke.

BANNER An act of contrition should do it.

ALAN It was a *joke*. I mean, he couldn't really . . . You wouldn't let him.

(*Silence*)

I'll tell him I'm sorry.

BANNER It was a very evil and wicked remark.

ALAN Blasphemous. I see that. I'll tell him.

BANNER He's waiting.

(ALAN *walks in from the deck, stopping to give one wild and wondering glance at* BANNER, *who does not respond, but ushers him to the cabin area, where* ARTHUR *waits. While*)

TONY (*as if to the sharks*) Well, I'm not going to be your dinner. I'll tell you that.

BANNER The sinner approaches your presence, high priest.

(*Goes back to his seat against the wall*)

ARTHUR Enter.

(ALAN *enters*)

ALAN I'm very sorry, high priest. I am truly sorry that I have sinned.

ARTHUR The god is angry.

ALAN I am truly——

ARTHUR I've told you before, sorrow is of no practical use without the intention of amendment.

ALAN I do intend it.

ARTHUR It is necessary at the beginning that there should be one among the Selected to doubt and rebel, so that his chastisement by the god should be remembered by the people.

ALAN I'm not rebelling, Arthur.

ARTHUR Not at the moment. No.

ALAN Never again.

ARTHUR Well, you are not to be blamed for it. You do no less in your way than we all do in ours. You express the will of the god. He has willed your doubt, because he wills your expiation.

ALAN What form would that take. . . . Arthur?

ARTHUR When the god came out of the sea just now, what did he want? It was not clear to me. Although I am close to the god—part of the god, Mr. Armitage—his intentions are not always clear, even to me. I did not

83

know what he would . . . I had thought foolishly that I was his only incarnation. Not true. Then he laid his hand on the raft, and I was powerless. It was the god himself.

ALAN The god Arthur?

ARTHUR In another form.

ALAN It couldn't have been . . . an anti-god?

ARTHUR No, or I should have prevailed. It was the god himself —made squid.

ALAN I should never have doubted it. I see that now.

ARTHUR Then you spoke, I struck you, and I knew.

ALAN What he wanted?

ARTHUR Yes.

ALAN And that is?

ARTHUR Sacrifice. A sign of our belief. An offering.

ALAN (*tentative*) We do sacrifice, high priest. We offer our first fruits to the god.

ARTHUR That is an act of devotion, not a sacrifice. It does not hurt us to give them. Though . . . 'first fruits'. . . . Yes, even from the mouth of an unbeliever, the god may speak. First fruits . . . the god's appearance in the likeness of a sea-creature . . . the delay in coming to land. . . . Iphigenia. . . . It all fits, Mr. Armitage. It is all of a piece.

ALAN What . . . did you think of sacrificing, Arthur?

ARTHUR What would you think most worthy?

ALAN Not me. *I'm* not worthy. I——

ARTHUR No.

ALAN —though I'm ready, of course, to do as the god wills.

ARTHUR Not you.

(*Pause*)

ALAN Later perhaps.

ARTHUR Perhaps.

ALAN I don't know what you had in mind, of course—what the god had in mind . . . who . . .

ARTHUR Why do you ask? It can make no difference. We are all equal in the eyes of the god.

(*Pause*)

84

ALAN It wouldn't be any of the women, of course. . . . I
      mean, the god would want them to . . . to multiply . . .
      to . . . (*rattled*) there are some of the women it couldn't
      possibly be! There are some—he'd want an
      unblemished body. A good body. Someone like
      Tony; he'd appreciate that. He'd want . . . Or if you
      thought Harold. . . . If you thought he might relish
      Harold. . . .

ARTHUR The mechanics of the thing might need a little
      arrangement. That is often the case in matters of
      religion, is it not?

ALAN None of the women.

ARTHUR I shall need your help. Since you have a penance to
      perform, that is convenient.

ALAN The god wouldn't want a pregnant woman. It's tabu.
      That's the last person he'd want.
      (*Pause*)

ARTHUR The pregnancy is much advanced.
      (*Pause*)

ALAN I have to go to the lavatory.

ARTHUR No, you don't.
      (*Pause*)

ARTHUR It would be better for the others not to know.

ALAN Eh?

ARTHUR A sacrifice need not be public to be effective. Only the
      will to give is important. Later on, the others would be
      told. That is the god's will.

ALAN But they'd notice. You couldn't. . . . It would cause
      grave resentment.

ARTHUR The confinement will take place in the temple.

ALAN (*desperately*) I have a revelation from the god.

ARTHUR (*carries straight on: overlapping*) We shall take the
      child.

ALAN The child?

ARTHUR An innocent life. Unblemished. For the god.

ALAN The child?

ARTHUR Yes.

ALAN Not . . . ?

85

ARTHUR Really, Mr. Armitage, have you been following me at all?

ALAN You're going to take the child? . . . Oh. . . . Oh yes, I had quite the wrong idea. Oh, that's wonderful. The child. . . . Yes. Yes, you do: you must: that's much better. I was quite wrong. I was very afraid, and quite wrong. The child. (*Now it hits him*) But how can you tell her?

ARTHUR There are anaesthetics in the first aid kit.

ALAN You'll say it died in childbirth?

ARTHUR It will be a secret we shall share with the god. Go now.
(ALAN *begins to go, but hesitates*)

ALAN There'll be . . . there'll be other children. It is best, isn't it? I mean, if *someone's* got to——

ARTHUR The god demands it.

ALAN (*going*) Yes. I see that.
(*He goes into the saloon area. He is dazed.* ASSISTANT *comes to* ARTHUR *and gives him the mask of the god. He sits gazing at it.* SONYA *is sitting with the others against the back wall.* ALAN *goes out on deck, ignores* TONY, *sits on a corner of the deck, crouched in a back-to-the-womb position.* TONY *looks at him. Meanwhile, as he has left the Main Cabin,* SONYA *rises from her chair, looking after him*)

SONYA Alan . . .
(*She follows him out on deck*)

SONYA Alan . . .

TONY Over there.
(*She joins* TONY. *Pause. She takes a step towards* ALAN)

SONYA Alan . . .

ALAN Go away.

SONYA (*small gesture to* TONY *to move away*) What's the matter, love?

ALAN (*hasn't looked round*) I saw that.
(TONY *looks from one to another, and hesitates*)

TONY I'll go in, then.

ALAN Why?
(*Pause*)

SONYA Go on in, Tone.

ALAN No.

SONYA (*to* TONY) Go on in.

ALAN (*shouts*) I said, no.

TONY (*to* SONYA) See you.

ALAN You don't want to leave us alone, Tony. Nobody ever leaves Sonya and me alone. You're the only one who's ever alone with Sonya.

SONYA (*to* TONY) Something's happened.

TONY Arthur's give him a bollocking.

ALAN Will you please stop talking *about* me? I'm not sick.

SONYA Tell me what's happened, then.

ALAN Just go away and leave me alone. Go away and do your exercises.

TONY (*to* SONYA) What's he on about?

SONYA Nothing. It's not important.

ALAN Ha!

TONY Stupid. You can't do exercises in the dark.

ALAN Can't you?

SONYA That's enough, Alan.

ALAN (*turns to* TONY) Tell me, Tony. Is Arthur God?

TONY I don't follow you.

ALAN Try. Just put one thought after another. It's a simple question. Is he a God? Do you obey him? Do you do his will?

SONYA I said, that's enough.

ALAN When you do your exercises, in the hold. Do you glory in it? A religious act?

TONY I don't know what you're on about. It's nothing to do with me, all that about religion. I just keep out of trouble.

(*Pause.* ALAN *gets up*)

ALAN You smug bastard! Arthur, and what he does to us: That's none of your business.

SONYA Tony, go inside.

ALAN What he does to us, and what he makes us do—you don't want to know. We can destroy ourselves, and as long as you do your bloody exercises down in the hold,

87

it doesn't matter.

SONYA What do you mean. 'What he *makes* us do?'

ALAN Do you think I don't know what sort of exercises you get up to?

SONYA (*loses temper*) No, you don't. You don't know any bloody thing.

(*Pause*)

TONY (*puzzled, to* SONYA) But it's not like that.

SONYA He's jealous.

TONY You never told him we——

ALAN She wouldn't tell me you didn't.

TONY (*to* SONYA) Why not?

SONYA He wouldn't have believed me. He won't believe you now.

(*Pause*)

TONY (*to* ALAN) You stupid sod! You don't know nothing about it. (*Pause*) I can't, if you want to know. (*Pause*) It's not that I don't fancy you, Sonn. I do, as a matter of fact.

SONYA Tony, this is not the time.

TONY But I just can't; that's all. I don't know why. If it was anyone else, it'd be funny. Laughable. When I was sixteen, the boys used to call me a sex maniac—I wore meself out like; it wasn't healthy. Then I saw one of them adverts in the papers, Why-be a Seven-Stone-Weakling? And I wanted to look good on the beach and that, and I thought doing exercises might take me mind off it, you know what I mean. And after a bit I found I wasn't interested no more. I thought it was the exercises done it. Being tired when I come home from the gym. And then I won all them prizes and had me picture on the cover of *Health and Strength*, and they was all after me—I could take me pick—and then when I did want to, I just couldn't.

SONYA Tony! Give over. Give over, eh?

TONY I've tried. There was one bird I fancied, she wouldn't believe it. She thought I was queer, and she could cure me, but I'm not. (*Pause*) So now you know. She's safe with me. Any bird's safe with me.

(*Pause*)

ALAN I'm sorry.

(SONYA *comes over to* TONY, *and kisses him*)

ALAN Jealousy! You imagine things. You get sick with it.

SONYA Sick!

ALAN I've been stupid.

SONYA You think nobody in the world exists but you. You're sick, and we've all got to die of it.

ALAN Sonn, we've got to get away from here.

SONYA Why? So that you can have me all to yourself again? I'll tell you now it won't work. First thing you know, you'll be saying, 'Who are you thinking about? Who did you dream about last night? Who do you think of when you kiss me?' I tell you, Alan Armitage, *I'm* the one who's sick, and it's time you remembered. I'm really sick. I get sick in the mornings. I vomit. I get so frightened, I'm sick. And I'm sick to death of you.

ALAN (*to* TONY) Tony, will *you* help us? He won't know. He won't know you helped. (*Pause*) Or you can come with us, if you like. He can come with us, Sonn.

(*Pause*)

TONY He gave you more than a bollocking.

SONYA What did he say to you in there?

ALAN He says the gods needs a sacrifice. He says that's why it came out of the sea. He says it wants a life— something new and innocent. He says when the baby is born, I have to help him sacrifice it to the god.

TONY And you said?

ALAN I was frightened. There was nobody to help me. What could I say?

TONY What did you say?

ALAN I said I would.

TONY You must be bloody mad.

(TONY *leaves them and walks straight into* ARTHUR's *room, miming throwing open the door*)

You!

(ARTHUR *begins to rise.* LECTURER *stops him*)

89

LECTURER Wait! The god protects you. He possesses you.
(ARTHUR *begins to put on the mask, but* TONY *grabs it, and throws it aside*)

ARTHUR He ho——

TONY Bloody kids' stuff.
(ASSISTANT *gives* ARTHUR *a piece of wood roughly in the shape of a knife.* ARTHUR *stabs at* TONY, *who cries out.* ARTHUR *escapes into Saloon area*)

ARTHUR Stop him. He is attacking the god.
(TONY *follows* ARTHUR, *clasping his shoulder. The other characters leave their places and come into the Saloon, where they watch*)

TONY This loony wants to kill little kids.

ARTHUR Mr. Armitage, you had no business to speak of this. Pray do your duty and protect me.

TONY You keep out of this. Bleeder pulled a knife on me. I'll fix him.

ARTHUR You will be helpless without me.

BANNER No one must interfere. It is for the god himself to settle.
(*Fight begins. They circle the table. But suddenly* ARTHUR *stops. It must appear as if the actor himself has forgotten his lines, and begun to feel ill. He leaves the fight and supports himself by first holding, then sitting on the table*)

ARTHUR No. I won't do it.
(*The others are surprised. They look at the* LECTURER *for guidance. They will remain still until their next movement is indicated, and they will always be looking at the* LECTURER, *wherever he may be*)

LECTURER What?

ARTHUR I won't do it. I know what will happen.

LECTURER You are Arthur. You know only what he knows. You cannot know the future.

ARTHUR I know what will happen. I was a student here.
(LECTURER *signs to* ASSISTANT *who goes out*)

LECTURER (*gentle*) If you know that, if you can remember that, then you know that you will survive it, and go free afterwards.

90

ARTHUR But Arthur will die. Tony will kill him. And I will feel
his death. His pain. And you make this happen. You
make me Arthur.

LECTURER You volunteered.

ARTHUR Yes, I volunteered for prison, too, do you remember?
We all volunteer. (*To* AUDIENCE) You volunteered to
attend this lecture. You volunteered to be students,
and those who are not students volunteered not to be.
We volunteer to obey in this community. We——

LECTURER Stop!

(ASSISTANT *has brought him a small glittering object,
probably a mirror set against a reflector and able to
revolve. He holds it up, compelling* ARTHUR *to watch*)
Now let me help you. Look at me. Watch. Watch now.
Submit now. Give me your will so that I can help you.
You want to obey because you are part of us. The
community wills it. You are the god Arthur, and you
must die for us all. You are the god, Arthur. You know
that now. You are the god.
(*Pause.* LECTURER *appears satisfied, and returns to his
place*)

ARTHUR No. I don't think so.

LECTURER What?

ARTHUR You are the god.

LECTURER I am Leading Lecturer in the History of the
Community, that is all. And you are Arthur Henderson.
The god Arthur.

ARTHUR There are no gods here but you. You are the
resurrection and the life. You reward obedience. But
I choose not to die, so you can keep your resurrection.

LECTURER Mr. Batch, pray kill the god.

ARTHUR I am not a god, I am a man. You are the god. You put
us here. You plan out the path we are to travel. But I
have free will. I can choose.

LECTURER You choose to be what you are. Arthur Henderson.
When this is over, you will be——

ARTHUR Reborn? But what if I choose to be Arthur in my own
way? If I choose to change your history? To be

                    Arthur, and kill Tony?

LECTURER You cannot alter history. It has already happened.

ARTHUR I can alter history because it *is* happening. (*Of the*
                    AUDIENCE) If I defy you, and kill Tony, their history
                    is altered.

                    (*Pause.* LECTURER *is considering the situation. He comes
                    to a decision*)

LECTURER Very well. If that is what you choose.

ARTHUR I do.

                    (LECTURER *holds him with his gaze. Perhaps clicks
                    fingers—something to suggest the re-establishment of the
                    hypnotic state*)

LECTURER You are Arthur. The knife is in your hand. . . Arthur.
                    Fight now. Fight for your life. Prove you are the leader,
                    and you can win.

ARTHUR I am Arthur. I have chosen. I will overcome.

                    (*He turns and rushes at* TONY. *A fight. Finally* TONY
                    throws ARTHUR *into the Sea Area, where he dies in
                    agony.* CAST *return to their seats upstage.* LECTURER
                    comes forward to speak to AUDIENCE)

LECTURER With the death of the God, they came at last to land,
                    and the New Society began. Next week we shall discuss
                    the early settlement, the period of chaos, and the
                    evolution of the Community Spirit. I do not wish you
                    to undervalue Arthur. The Community always uses
                    what is good in a man, and in the early Minutes of the
                    New Society you will find the source of many of the
                    Community Rules, just as the very first Community
                    Leader was the son whom Muriel Otterdale bore to
                    Arthur after his death. In the case of the criminal who
                    presented Arthur, you were able to witness the effects
                    of advanced individualism, which made him as we now
                    discover, a bad subject for hypnosis, and caused him
                    more pain than was strictly necessary. However, as you
                    saw, in the end the course of history was not changed.
                    Arthur was killed by Tony, and after this prisoner has
                    been revived, we shall continue treating him so as to
                    reclaim him for the community in time. (*To*

ASSISTANT) Revive him.

(ASSISTANT *comes to* ARTHUR, *bending over his body.*
LECTURER *goes to* CAST)

You have come to land now.

BANNER Land! Land, Muriel!

MURIEL I wonder how we shall go on there, then.

(ASSISTANT *has been unable to revive* ARTHUR. *Worried,
he comes to the* LECTURER *and whispers something*)

LECTURER What? Impossible?

MURIEL I wonder how we shall go on there, then.

(LECTURER *makes a swift examination of* ARTHUR. *Then,
shaken, he addresses the* AUDIENCE)

LECTURER This prisoner is dead. You will realize that this is no
part of the intention of the lecture. We cure criminals:
we do not kill them. The community does not, and will
not allow waste of any sort. Consequently it is
clear that the man himself chose to—(*catches himself:
realizes what he is saying*)—that the man chose his
own death.

MURIEL I wonder how we shall go on there, then. I wonder how
we shall go on there, then.

LECTURER There will be no questions. The lecture is over.

(CAST *leave.* MURIEL *continues to repeat her line until and
after she is off the stage. Effect is of a gramophone record
which has stuck.* ASSISTANTS *carry the body of* ARTHUR
offstage)

MURIEL I wonder how we shall go on there, then. (*Repeats*)

LECTURER You will not discuss what has happened.

(LECTURER *leaves the stage*)

END OF ACT THREE